Maxima Moralia

This book highlights the problem of one-dimensional, reductionistic life of the modern individual. An expression of crisis in our world, it discusses the imperative need to have a more comprehensive, non-reductionist life where the Other is incorporated, especially the relationship between the Other and the Self, based on virtues such as love, empathy, equality, and compassion.

The volume sheds light on how the world has forgone the art of living for a mutilated sense of well-being, the rise of conformity and complacency in human thought, and the lack of democratic dissent and citizenry responsibility in our contemporary societies, which is now characterized by mass immaturity, propelled by a process of thoughtlessness. It discusses how humans need to be aware of the life they lead, to think about Otherness of the Other not just as another virtue but also as a crucial element in the survival of humanity, for people to coexist with the world around them as equals. Furthermore, it advocates meaningful and thoughtful existence, in touch with the Nature we coexist with, to ensure that humanity is not robbed of its noble spirit as we live to survive in our techno-capitalist societies.

An introspective read, this book will be of great interest to scholars and researchers of moral and ethical philosophy, political philosophy, and political science.

Ramin Jahanbegloo is an Iranian–Canadian philosopher. He is presently the executive director of the Mahatma Gandhi Centre for Nonviolence and Peace Studies and the vice-dean of the School of Law at Jindal Global University, Sonipat, India. He is the winner of the Peace Prize from the United Nations Association in Spain (2009) for his extensive academic work in promoting dialogue among cultures and his advocacy for nonviolence. More recently, he is the winner of the Josep Palau i Fabre International Essay Prize. Some of his most recent publications are *Gadflies in the Public Space* (2016), *The Decline of Civilization* (2017), *Letters to a Young Philosopher* (2017), *On Forgiveness and Revenge* (2017), and *The Global Gandhi: Essays in Comparative Political Philosophy* (2018).

Maxima Moralia

Meditations on the Otherness of the Other

Ramin Jahanbegloo

LONDON AND NEW YORK

First published 2022
by Routledge
4 Park Square, Milton Park, Abingdon, Oxon OX14 4RN

and by Routledge
605 Third Avenue, New York, NY 10158

Routledge is an imprint of the Taylor & Francis Group, an informa business

© 2022 Ramin Jahanbegloo

British Library Cataloguing-in-Publication Data
A catalogue record for this book is available from the British Library

Library of Congress Cataloging-in-Publication Data
A catalog record has been requested for this book

ISBN: 978-1-032-25693-1 (hbk)
ISBN: 978-1-032-27436-2 (pbk)
ISBN: 978-1-003-29277-7 (ebk)

DOI: 10.4324/9781003292777

Typeset in Times New Roman
by Apex CoVantage, LLC

To Don Mario Aguilar, for his exceptional meaningfulness and unparalleled empathy in the battlefield of life

Contents

Introduction

This book is the expression of a crisis in our world. It is a crisis in several senses. From a civilizational standpoint, we are living in an age of mediocrity. This is an age of imbecility and infantilism. It is an age of what Kant called "self-incurred minority." This minority is expressed by the inability of today's individuals to make use of their understanding and to think for themselves. As a matter of fact, in these troubled times, the art of questioning has been replaced by the rise of conformity and complacency among the citizens of the world. In other words, the contemporary world is characterized by mass immaturity and propelled by a process of thoughtlessness. The second expression of the crisis that humanity is living at a global level is the shortcomings of democratic passion and citizenry responsibility in our contemporary societies. Consequently, democracy in the 21st century has ceased to be a way of life. Democracy, to be worthy of obedience, must be structured so that every citizen can question and disobey unjust laws and institutions. However, the truth is that the corporate mindset which has conquered the economic, political, and academic institutions around the globe has, at the same time, destroyed the disobedient spirit of democracy. As a result, dissent is no more a moral and political imperative in liberal societies; it has become a cultural luxury, which is practised in the private spaces. The third and last aspect of the global crisis mentioned is the social and individual degradations of the moral of compassion and empathy among the peoples of the Earth. We are living in a world where the ideas of success and utility have replaced those of compassion and empathy. Therefore, what we call "well-being" as a mutilated meaning of life has replaced the art of living. While life has become meaningless, death is no more than statistics. Humanity is living a civilizational incapacity to generate a common horizon of shared values. And this is a handicap which goes beyond human civilizations. It touches the essence of life itself and the relation of humans with Nature. We, humans, have lost all contact with the biodiversity of the planet Earth. For the first time in our human history, empathy and compassion are

DOI: 10.4324/9781003292777-1

no more parts of our civilizational upbringing. We live on the planet Earth without knowing why we share this planet with a diversity of plants and animals. This state of meaningless and thoughtless existence not only robs humanity of its nobility of spirit but also makes humans totally indifferent to the Otherness of the Other. Let us not forget that the acknowledgement of the Otherness of the Other is actually accompanied by an awareness of Man's fallibility and the impossibility to maintain itself unflinchingly in an unquestionable and unaccountable intellectual stance. This is where the democratic paideia and the exercise of empathetic pluralism and compassionate friendship in regard to the non-human world goes hand in hand with a permanent struggle against the spirit of violence and its unethical and utilitarian expressions in our democracies.

The liability to think about the Otherness of the Other is not just another virtue in the catalog of humanity morality. It is a crucial element in the survival enterprise of humanity. We do not live as humans to think the Otherness of the Other, but, on the contrary, we think the Otherness of the Other in order to continue to survive as human beings. It's time for humanity to start coexisting with the world around it as equals; otherwise, the world will continue not only to be inaccessible to the human race but also of no significance to it. It would be a shame and an indignity for humanity to continue to bless the lies with which its lives while it is cursed by them. Perhaps it's time for us to accept the fact that the iron necessity of our techno-capitalist world is neither iron nor necessary. In the final analysis, the meaning of life is in life itself. If we do not understand and respect the Otherness of life, ultimately there would be no life at all.

1 Age of Mediocrity

1

Our age is essentially one of mediocrity without passion. Nowadays not even desperation can give meaning to our lives. The word "success" has become our banner, along with many other meaningless concepts. In the present age, of course, it would be out of the question to think. The motto of today's world is: we were born not to think but to succeed.

2

To be sure, the present age is ridiculously false in its pretensions. Those who live in this era are safely dead and yet have the right to live like zombies. They do not mainly seek to add to humanity's wisdom, but what they most want is to live without thinking about life itself.

3

Strangely, we die no more *with* death but *from* the ignorance of death. In an age with no passion, even the value of death is misplaced. The age of romantic or heroic deaths is past. The present is the age of individuals who die without knowing *why* and for *what* they die.

4

Where neither excellence nor exemplarity is in the game, any light-hearted move in life is like swimming in shallow waters. It's only when our feet don't touch the ground that we might end in the inwardness of wisdom.

DOI: 10.4324/9781003292777-2

5

Those who feel predestined to lead and not to listen in the world will be pushed down by history itself. Those who do not listen to the logic of history should see to it that in the process they are not thrown in the abyss of history.

6

Supposing techno-science can make us eternal-what then? It is a fundamental truth of human nature that humankind is incapable of admiring anything permanently, including eternity. Human nature lives with boredom.

7

The further it is internalized the more clearly does boredom become a poison that kills with little dosages in a long period of time. As a result, all that is despicable comes to the forefront of one's life.

8

One cannot be loved as long as one is still execrable, except by those who credit others with their hate and contempt.

9

To what extent can we talk about love in our age of mediocrity? Perhaps the misinterpretation of love is so great that it keeps us from loving and being loved.

10

Even a simple kiss is corrupted by our political correctness. The more sanitized is the love that we teach our children, the less they know about love and how to seduce their senses.

11

What can love say where there is no Beloved Community? The paradox of love is that its true ground is itself. In other words, love is the question and the answer.

12

Even if I possess the whole world and I have no love, I am nothing. Nothing is closer to our essence than love which is the foundation of our being. As Thomas Merton puts it correctly, "Love is our true destiny."

13

What humanity needs is a genuine revolution of love. Only loving can change its mode of thinking and create a fundamental change in human society. In reality, love is the spiritual force which gives meaning to human life.

14

Love, therefore, is the power of self-transformation. That is perhaps the main reason why love is a disobeying and dissenting force. To love is to be alive and to have the courage to redefine life.

15

Meaninglessness is an expression of the absence of love in the present age. It is an absolute threat to human civilization. It deprives humanity from its courage to exist. But humanity needs to remind itself of what it has lost or is continuously losing.

16

Love is the basis of the courage to exist. Only this courage can fight against meaninglessness and the mediocrity which follows. If life and death become meaningless, then the anxiety of fate can be defeated only by the courage to exist.

17

The paradox of every life is that it has the power to disobey and negate its own meaninglessness. The act of transcending meaninglessness is in itself a meaningful act of dissent.

18

Dissent is essential to understanding how humanity can liberate itself from the grip of meaninglessness and mediocrity. As such, there is no meaningful living without dissenting.

19

If life is an act of dissent, then the courage to exist is the art of being alerted about the Otherness of the Other. To recognize the Otherness of the Other is to accept the courage and the patience of being in fellowship, even in the grip of meaninglessness and conformity.

20

The courage to exist is not an issue of solipsism. On the contrary, it shows that each one of us needs to participate in the affirmation of the Otherness of the Other. Every act of courage to exist is the manifestation of the Other and the recognition of its Otherness.

21

Love is the vital force which marks the presence of the Other in the world. The courage to exist is rooted in the love of the Other as an experience of self-transformation. Consequently, the courage to exist as oneself is always accompanied by the courage to recognize the existence of the Other as Otherness.

22

If the courage to exist is the courage to think oneself in the world and to self-affirm oneself in life, then the courage to be as oneself is also the courage to mark the presence of the Otherness of the Other in the world.

23

Since life is neither static nor monistic, then it has a great inclination for plurality, diversity, and change. By which we mean that life is nothing but modes of being, heterogeneous, and dissimilar. Thus, the Otherness of the Other is nothing but a different Self which emerges from within the same world.

24

Curiously the recognition of the Otherness of the Other, as the presence of plurality in the world, turns the courage to exist into a moral capital. Underlying this moral capital resides the use of nonviolence as a power of compassion and love. This, in a sense, echoes what Mahatma Gandhi calls *Satyagraha.*

2   The Power of Agape

25

Satyagraha is the moral authority to say "No" to homogeneity and to say "Yes" to plurality and diversity. It is a commitment to nonviolence and truth in the name of the Otherness of the Other.

26

Martin Luther King, Jr. said:

> Compassion and nonviolence help us to see the enemy's point of view, to hear his questions, to know his assessment of ourselves. For from his view we may indeed see the basic weaknesses of our own condition, and if we are mature, we may learn and grow and profit from the wisdom of the brothers who are called the opposition.

27

Let us not forget that in times of darkness, nonviolence is the *maxima moralia* of humanity. Thinking nonviolence in a world of meaninglessness that would dismiss and banish all forms of originality and independent mindedness is the only way to restore the nobility and greatness of human spirit.

28

It is the characteristic of our unphilosophical age to cling firmly to violence. Violence is a truth that is recognized best by complacent and conformist minds, because the seductive power of violence exists only for the mobs. Mahatma Gandhi did not surrender to the fanaticism of the mobs. As he underlined: "A democratic organization has to dare to do the right at all cost.

DOI: 10.4324/9781003292777-3

He who panders to the weaknesses of a people degrades both himself and the people, and leads them not to democratic but mob rule."

29

Mediocrity as the expression of a threatening meaninglessness is the absence of courage to exist and to think about existence. Mediocrity is mastered by fear, and therefore, it loses the zest for living. Mediocre men lose easily the will to live.

30

Nonviolence invites us constantly to hold back the flood of mediocrity and meaninglessness and to struggle for the nobility of spirit and moral excellence. This fidelity to the human spirit and to the moral essence of life is the first and most essential nature of nonviolence.

31

There is nothing that expresses moral excellence than cultivating a conscience which disobeys injustice and requests freedom for the Other. To put it in concrete terms, a *satyagrahi* is one who seeks responsibility for the Other, while recognizing itself responsible for the welfare of others.

32

The manifestation of love in nonviolence is, therefore, not an expression of a simple "mode d'être" but the quality of a radical view of reality. True nonviolence is not the absence of revolutionary change, because it is a true revolution of values.

33

When it comes to change, love of the world comes always first, the effort to change oneself comes second. Only then, we can transform the world.

34

Changing the world isn't everything, by thinking and trying change is. The aim here is not to defeat the world but try to perfect one's character in life.

35

This is as much a wager as Pascal's. For Pascal, if God does not exist, the agnostic loses little by believing in Him and gains a little by not believing. But if God does exist, the agnostic gains eternal life by believing in Him and loses a great deal by not believing. Being the vanguard of a new humanity is neither a loss nor a gain for conformists and those who fear change. The great question is not whether the change will come or not but whether humanity has the choice to change.

36

We will never have a true change in the world until human beings in all cultures and traditions of thought recognize that a true revolution of values is needed. Ultimately, humanity cannot reach peace and harmony through ambition and pride. Ambition without compassion is like a tree with no roots in the ground.

37

Nothing is more exemplary than a character with strong roots in an independent will. The courage to exist is a virtue which cannot survive without the need to be rooted. According to Simone Weil: "Whoever is uprooted himself uproots others. Whoever is rooted himself doesn't uproot others."

38

The function of education is to teach a human being to build a character and to be rooted. It must be remembered that the greatest threat to all genuine Otherness of the Other in our world are individuals and institutions who believe that violence is an answer to our global problems.

39

If humanity is bound tightly together as an undivided family, then any form of violence will drive out peace and solidarity. But peace can only be achieved by understanding the Other and its Otherness.

40

We can only understand a cat by its *catness* and a dog by its *dogness*. The same goes for a tree, an ocean, and a mountain. There is no true communication or communion with the other living being without an *understanding of* and a *compassion for* its Otherness.

41

What is the telos of Otherness? It's the fulfilment of the Other. As Angelus Silesius writes majestically: "The Rose because she is a rose does blossom, she never asks why."

42

To understand the *roseness* of the rose is only possible because we are unfulfilled without this understanding. Aiming for the Otherness of the Other is aiming for wholeness.

43

We fulfil ourselves by the love of the Other. Love is part of the entry into the Otherness of the Other. Love is important because it masters fear. This is the higher law of all spiritual men and women.

44

Martin Luther King, Jr. distinguishes between three forms of love which are central to the human experience: "*eros*," "*philia*," and most significant of all "*Agape*." According to King, "*Agape* means nothing sentimental or basically affectionate; it means understanding, redeeming goodwill for all men, an overflowing love which seeks nothing in return." Only *Agape* love is able to understand and to empathize with the Otherness of the Other.

45

In the lifelong journey of the Self and the Other, we need to reach into ethic of love. The existential courage to exist and the *Agapeic* love of the Other could help us to eliminate social and political evils of humanity.

46

We find this weariness with the evil throughout the history of humanity. But, in our age, things are different. We have become so familiar with the evil that we have forgotten what it really is. The awful fact is that though humankind seeks to avoid the evil, it always finds a reason to get involved with it. As such, human beings not only accept the evil, but they even also go as far as to sacrifice their lives for it.

47

As it was said previously, if meaninglessness and ambition for success are the two arch enemies of humanity in today's world, then the only possible conclusion to this is that human dignity and the nobility of human spirit are endangered by the evil of mediocrity.

48

Pascal is right to say: "Nothing is as approved as mediocrity, the majority has established it and it fixes its fangs on whatever gets beyond it either way." In other words, mediocrity is the highest expression of moral relativism and cultural infantilism in our civilization.

49

No wonder why our world has degenerated into moral chaos and each generation more than the precedent one is suffering from an acute infantilism. If Kant was among us today, he would have been surprised by the number of people who make known publicly their opinions without really having a moral engagement about what they publicize. This public use of the pen is no more a freedom and a right; it is a bad taste exhibitionism.

50

Kant defines Enlightenment as the human being's emergence from its self-incurred minority. He uses the German word "*Unmündigkeit*" which is also translated as "immaturity." Yet, he is not making use of this concept in the legal sense but as an inability to make use of one's own understanding.

3   The Art of Maturity

51

One of the salient features of our age is the growing ethical and political immaturity of citizens around the world. Never mind the social turmoil that we see from time to time around the world, but on the deeper level, techno-scientific progress has not made humanity more alert about its ills and challenges.

52

What is needed urgently is a spiritual Enlightenment. This is not a dynamic of religious inwardness but a matter of moral adjustment of the entire human family. It's a pre-condition to all future project of critical self-rule.

53

However, not everything that is publicized as "spiritual" comes up to the moral standards demanded by nonviolence. True nonviolence demands excellence, exemplarity, and the courage to self-transform. Gandhi describes it as a "power of resistance" and as an art of not harbouring hatred in one's heart.

54

This brings us back to the idea of compassion for the Other accompanied by an empathetic effort to understand the Otherness of the Other. Moreover, those who have compassion must have the ability to forgive. Those who cannot forgive must live with the perpetual fear of the others.

DOI: 10.4324/9781003292777-4

55

Consequently, as Gandhi points out, the noblest way of living is to struggle for the common good of humanity. As Gandhi asserts: "There is no limit to extending ours service to our neighbors across state-made frontiers." In that sense, Gandhi invites us to transcend narrow-mindedness, selfishness, and exclusiveness.

56

Empathy, undoubtedly, is life's most important existential task. Empathy is not just *a sense of curiosity* but mostly also *a mode of caring* about the Otherness of the Other. Socially, one human is curious about another, but only morally would a person care for another person.

57

For Heidegger, *care for* (*Sorge*) is a form of *concern and anxiety for* others, directed toward the future. This anxiety about the future is at the same time a desire to attend to the world. Heidegger most certainly remains excessively susceptible to the philosophical structures of Western subjectivism and thus undermines the non-Western dimensions of *care*.

58

Let us take for example, the ethics of care and empathy in the African culture of *Ubuntu*. According to Archbishop Desmond Tutu, "*Ubuntu* speaks particularly about the fact that you can't exist as a human being in isolation. It speaks about our interconnectedness." In other words, empathy is walking with others on a tightrope. In a nutshell, the ethics of empathy is to look within oneself while looking at the Other. That is to say, at a more fundamental level, cultures and nations are not isolated entities, because they all play a special role in the making of human history.

59

Empathy is the sole source of morality against all forms of monism and exclusionary belief systems. In order to appreciate the plurality of lived human experiences, we need an appeal to a moral grounding which could structure itself on both the imperfection and the cultural diversity of the human species. If, as Isaiah Berlin points out correctly, pluralities are made possible in life by the flexibility, fragility, and imperfectability of human nature, then the desire for empathy goes hand in hand with an ethical maturity *à la Kant*, which is marked by an existential appreciation of the Otherness of the Other.

60

If the world is a realm of uncertainties and diversities, then life does not provide us with ready-made answers. Therefore, no one person, culture, or nation could pretend to have a re-established response to the enigma of history. The perennial search for the meaning of life cannot be found in a logocentric or theocentric system of principles, since life is un-ended quest for meaning. As Herzen puts it: "the ultimate goal of life is life itself."

61

This willingness to engage with the Otherness of the Other creates a space of dialogue in which an interaction between different horizons of thought becomes possible. To follow the path of Isaiah Berlin, we can say that by approaching the Otherness of the Other, we realize "there is a plurality of values which men can and do seek, and that these values differ."

62

This, indeed, is the principal lesson that one can take from the study of human civilizations. As a matter of fact, historical cultures despite their differences possess many commonalities that enable mutual understanding. The most important among these is the human capacity for intercultural understanding and empathy. As we can see, here the intercultural empathy at the level of an interaction among nations adds up to the Agape love at the level of individual exchange.

63

The key point here is a moral common ground that provides the evidence of the universality of values and which identifies us as an undivided family. Consequently, universal values are universally shared by all cultures and nations, not only because they are humanly recognizable but also because they constitute a moral standpoint for human intercultural plurality.

64

Tagore understood the logic of cultural pluralism better than any other thinker in 20th century. For him, cultural pluralism was not founded on a religious idea, but it was more of a philosophical attitude based on the rejection of moral and cultural monism. Tagore explicitly denied the intellectual position that there was only one way of life. As a result, he believed that human civilization was not established on the moral and ontological superiority of one culture over others.

65

Tagore defined cultural pluralism as the ontological self-expression of humankind as a cultural animal. That is why in Tagore's pluralist philosophy cultural coexistence goes hand with an inter-civilizational symbiosis. In a letter to Foss Westcott, Tagore wrote, "Believe me, nothing would give me greater happiness than to see the people of the West and the East march in a common crusade against all that robs the human spirit of its significance."

66

Tagorean vision is based on the very fact that no culture is a monolithic, rigid, and static entity which could develop itself in isolation and without contact with other cultures. In other words, each one of us can cut across the boundaries of race, religion, and nationality and engage in a dialogical understanding of other cultures. That is to say, empathetic pluralism encourages and promotes the intercultural dialogue.

67

What is so fundamental in Tagore's philosophy of the Otherness of the Other is his severe criticism of nationalistic passions and fervours. Tagore, more than any of his contemporaries in the East or in the West, insists on the readiness of each culture to adopt a self-critical posture in regard to its nationalistic self-interests. Actually, Tagore denounces nationalism as a form of "sectarian arrogance" that magnifies the self of a nation without understanding the higher ideal of humanity.

68

If this higher ideal of humanity can be defined as the Otherness of the Other, then one can find in Rabindranath Tagore its great poet and in Mahatma

Gandhi its exemplary practitioner. When one reads Tagore, the immediate impression is that he is writing for our dark times. He says: "The call has come to every individual in the present age to prepare himself and his surroundings for this dawn of a new era, when man shall discover his soul in the spiritual unity of all human beings."

69

Tagore's conception of cultural pluralism is refreshing and inspiring, because he does not envision an uncritical affirmation of all cultural values and he does not require a suspension of moral judgement in the process of a dialogue among cultures. Once again, Tagore elevates the universal value of education as an institution of not only listening and learning but also developing individuals into channels of empathy and dialogue.

70

Tagore is fully aware of the state of education in contemporary times and criticizes the loss of spiritual meaning and moral excellence in an educational process which has become purely materialistic and utilitarian. He underlines:

> Great civilizations in the East as well as in the West, have flourished in the past because they produced food for the spirit of man for all time; they had their life in the faith in ideals, the faith which is creative. These great civilizations were at last run to death by men of the type of our precocious schoolboys of modern times, smart and superficially critical, worshippers of self, shrewd bargainers in the market of profit and power, efficient in their handling of the ephemeral, who presumed to buy human souls with their money and threw them into their dustbins when they had been sucked dry, and who, eventually, driven by suicidal forces of passion, set their neighbours' houses on fire and were themselves enveloped by the flame.

71

Following Tagore, we can say that an educational age is an age of listening, learning, and sharing; ours is an age of noise, egoism, and imbecility. Kierkegaard adds to this the following: "In the present age a rebellion is, of all things, the most unthinkable. Such an expression of strength would seem ridiculous to the calculating intelligence of our times." Kierkegaard steps here in the shoes of Kant and repeats with him the battle cry of the Enlightenment, *Sapere Aude*: "Have the courage to use your own reason!" or put differently, "Have the courage to think for yourself!"

4   *Paideia* and Epistemic Humility

72

If there is one thing that the Greeks and the Romans knew well was that education is not about becoming rich and powerful. What the ancient Athenians called "*paideia*" was a long process of character development and civic education. Thus, as Cornelius Castoriadis reminds us sharply and shrewdly,

> As the current evolution of *paideia* is not wholly irrelevant to the inertia and the social and political passivity characteristic of our world today, a renaissance of its vitality, will be indissociable from a great new politico-social movement that will reactivate democracy and will give it at once the form and the contexts the idea of democracy requires, should it take place.

73

It goes without saying that the crisis of politics in today's world goes hand in hand with the crisis of "*paideia*." There is no such thing as "*paideia*" or even a simple civic education in contemporary societies. Education has no more an emancipative task in the 21st century. Students go to college and university to graduate with a diploma that they hang on the wall of their offices, not to become autonomous and to learn to think for themselves. Otherwise, humanity is experiencing the end of "*humanitas*."

74

Oxford Dictionary defines "*humanitas*" as "a humanistic approach to the problems of the human condition." It is in this relation that we have Terence's famous affirmation "*homo sum; humani nil a me alienum puto*" (I am a human being and I reckon nothing human alien to me.) makes sense. Here

DOI: 10.4324/9781003292777-5

humanitas refers to a human fellowship which is learned through culture and civic education. But *humanitas* also goes hand in hand with what the Romans called *sensus communis* (a shared experience of reality).

75

This inclusive use of the term *humanitas* reminds us that education always refers to the commonality of humankind and to something learned about humans. But *humanitas* also notifies us that the entire human race can be taught to be compassionate. This is often expressed by evoking the difference between "barbarous" (the person who has no mercy) and "civilized" (the compassionate). *Humanitas*, then, has a close connection with the appreciation of the characteristics of the Other.

76

If *humanitas* is self-educated humanity, then the end of *humanitas* brings with it the end of a certain human civilization. A civilization in which, as Castoriadis underlines, *paideic* education "involves becoming conscious that the polis is also oneself and that its fate also depends upon one's mind, behaviour, and decisions; in other words, it is participation in political life."

77

One can go back and study John Dewey's vision of democratic education in relation with the eclipse of the twin concepts of *paideia* and *humanitas* in contemporary culture. At the heart of this concern is Dewey's idea of thinking as a process of engagement with doubt. If we embrace this view seriously, we come to realize that the process of learning is always connected to the emergence of critical thinking and questioning. But today's education is void of any form of questioning. Young men and women do not learn to question reality but to obey and reproduce it.

78

However, questioning is a transformative action in the world. A person who questions is disobedient, anti-conformist, and non-complacent. Here the spirit of dissent is measured by an aspiration to moral courage that enables all citizens to think and to act otherwise. But since every education is a form of dialogue with the world, then the Self can recognize in this relationship the Otherness of the Other and share experiences of a common reality with it. Therefore, living is experiencing the art of dialogue – a dialogue between the individual choice and the necessity of the world.

79

As Paulo Freire argues,

> Human beings did not come into the world only to adapt themselves to the situations they find. It is as if we received a mission to re-create the world constantly. This is human existence. By being historical beings, we are creative beings.

But there is no creativity without questioning, and there is no questioning without an interrogative character-building. Gandhi understood correctly that the goal of education is character-building. He used to say that, "The end of all knowledge must be building up of character." Gandhi felt that true education calls for the self-realization of the individual. Here we need to distinguish between the development of character by the education and individualism. For Gandhi, there is no moral aim in individualism. That is why individualism is a total neglect of the Otherness of the Other.

80

Gandhi believed that "True education should result not in the material power, but in spiritual-force." Where can this force come from in a divided world, threatened by the decline of democratic practice, ecological disasters, regional conflicts, rise of populist regimes, and the growth of mediocrity in our everyday life? The answer to this question is not easy. However, if humanity feels responsible for its future, then individuals and nations should come together to strengthen the hopes without which human race would have collapsed in its long and difficult journey.

81

The times ahead of us are of a very difficult nature. We need to change our habits of mind and patterns of behaviour in order to protect humanity against all its evils, safeguard democratic mode of thinking, and rescue the planet Earth. It goes without saying that the future destiny of humanity is based on its character. "*Character is destiny.*" This quote from the ancient Greek philosopher Heraclitus is worth repeating. Character is that on which the destiny of humanity is built. Humanity is nothing without character. What we call progress is nothing if it is not accompanied with a nobility of character. As such, in the last analysis, it is not techno-science but the resources of character which will decide the future of humanity.

82

It is wrong to imagine that science and technology could save humanity from its evils and find a solution to the lack of harmony in the world. Technology, by essence, is incapable of providing answers to the situation of meaninglessness and mediocrity in which humanity finds itself. The great technological revolution has lead human race to abundance and success, but it has not provided humankind with spiritual depth and peace. Thomas Merton, the American Trappist monk, adds: "If you are too obsessed with success, you will forget to live." The epistemological arrogance of techno-science has deprived us of the art of living.

83

What we need today is a sense of epistemic humility, which can learn not only from humankind's biological and ontological fragility but also from the fact that we are in need of companionship and recognition. In other words, this epistemic humility can make us conscious about the fact that humanity is a collective survival enterprise. Every human society has a common responsibility to provide security and sustainability for the life of future generations. This is not an utilitarian effort but a step towards the development of a global consciousness which re-orients humankind in the direction of cosmic interconnectedness and world solidarity.

84

The battle for the future of humankind is not won in grand technological corporations but in the hearts of human beings, which are less diverted and distracted than their minds. As Pascal says: "If man were happy, the less he were diverted the happier he would be like the saints and God." Being unable to embrace the meaning of life, contemporary subject decided, in order to be happy, not to think about life itself and divert its concentration towards mass communication technologies. As such, for a corporate mindset, life and death are taken for *given* and not admitted as *task*s of the mind.

85

Let us be clear, the technological revolution in the past 100 years was not accompanied by a spiritual change. Modern Man has been wandering in obscurity, because it suffers from a spiritual failure, while it cannot throw light upon its future. However, humankind has become totally a stranger to the logic of life. Human beings take no more the pleasure of admiring

Nature without having the urge to conquer it. Mountains are not for climbing and oceans do not represent scuba diving tanks. The difference between a corporate leader and a Buddhist monk is that the latter can live in peace and harmony with the Himalayas without feeling the need to conquer the summit. For a Buddhist monk, the Other is represented by its Otherness, not by its utility and profitability.

86

As His Holiness the Dalai Lama mentions: "The planet does not need more successful people. The planet desperately needs more peacemakers, healers, restorers, storytellers, and lovers of all kinds." Being a stranger to Nature and biodiversity, Modern Man has lost its experience of thinking and mediating about life and death. Yet, the civilizational testament reminds us that for long centuries, living was an experience that was accompanied by a sense of meaning and sacredness. But today, neither life nor death are sacred. We consider them no more as objects of contemplation capable of mystical transfiguration but as individual events with no meaningful essence.

87

In a letter dated 23 October 1923 to Abbé Breuil, Pierre Teilhard de Chardin writes: "The longer I live the more certain I am that individual events count for nothing; all that really matters is devotion to something bigger than ourselves." What can be bigger than life in comparison with individual existence? How can we give meaning to life otherwise than by approaching through individual existence? Awareness of the Otherness of the Other is something which is given in immediate experience. We need to look at the world and find out its character. This is how we can discover the courage of existence. To paraphrase Alfred Whitehead: "The courage to exist is what a human being does with its solitariness."

88

To exist is the courage to affirm the world or to affirm the existence of the Other in the world. The affirmation of the Otherness of the Other is a ground for one's self-awareness. This is how humanity asserts itself in us against all that negates humanity in our individuality. History is in this sense the epic of the individual becoming humanity. The essence of history is found in all human beings, though it becomes manifest only in some. But history is always hopeful, always patient. As long as we do not conquer history, truth is an unattainable horizon.

5 The Otherness of the Other

89

But why do we need the Otherness of the Other? Because we want "humaneness." As Confucius asserts: "Is humaneness really so far away? If we ourselves wanted humaneness, then humaneness would arrive." That is to say, humaneness never comes into being with abstinence; it comes with effort and struggle. Humaneness is not a blank idea; it is a mode of action.

90

Humaneness is always at the beginning. The end to achieve is to attain the Otherness of the Other. As we say in Latin: *Finis Origine Pendet* (The end depends upon the beginning). Humaneness is not about following the Other. It is a response to the challenge of life. Here arises a responsibility which implies a revolution of values.

91

Living wisely is the greatest revolution of values. However, wisdom is not something that we can acquire in one night and spread around us. It is a process of learning the world which only starts when we start unlearning how we think in everyday life. Wisdom is that which transmits to us a sense of the eternal, a sense which is beyond the merely everydayness. It is because there is a meaning which is beyond the everydayness of human world that we are able to attain it as an expression of the universal. Human being has the capacity in it to overcome the mediocrity of everydayness. The truth is that the amplitude of existence is in the creative life.

DOI: 10.4324/9781003292777-6

92

Creation is possible only when there is freedom from self-centredness, envy, and jealousy. Creation is the way of understanding the Otherness of the Other. It needs patience and a calm mind, but more than anything else, it needs courage. As Camus affirms beautifully, "To create today is to create dangerously." Hence, the first step toward creativity is to understand one's bondage. Creation is only possible when our body and mind are not slaves of the logic of everydayness. Creation cannot be conformity and complacency. Though all humans have a common sense and perception of the world, they each have a different creative approach to what is unfinished in the world.

93

There is no need of proclaiming whether creative wisdom must flee from the unfinished in the world or challenge it. Creation is neither complete rejection nor complete acceptance of what is unfinished in the world. The aim of creative wisdom is to advocate the art of living beyond the legislation of good and evil. This is why life cannot serve fanaticism. Tyrants know this better than anyone else, that is why they hate life. Life is not an idea; it is a difficult conclusion which needs courage. Therefore, the courage to exist is a revolt against a Being which has no Becoming.

94

The Otherness of the Other is the Becoming of Being. There must be vulnerability of Being to have Becoming. The Self turns toward the Other, because it cannot remain enclosed and insensitive to the art of living. The Self cancels the tyrant within itself and turns toward the Other. The Self knows that it is condemned to live and die with the Other. It is interesting how the Self and the Other can create a community of hope against the fatality of Being that closes in upon them. Yet, it is fallacious to think that religion is essential for a community of hope to exist. Many benefactors of the human history were perfect agnostics. Let us listen to what Swami Vivekananda has to say about Gautama Buddha. He declares:

> I would like to see a moral man like Gautama Buddha who did not believe in a Personal God or a personal soul, never asked even about them but was a perfect agnostic, and yet was ready to lay down his life for anyone, and worked all his life for the good of all.

95

The true task of the Self and the Other is not to desert the battle of Becoming. That is the condition under which creative wisdom is possible. Neither wisdom nor creation are simple repetitions of reality. They are compassionate revolts against the reality of a stagnant world. If revolt has any meaning in this world, it means nothing but the recognition of the Otherness of the Other, which cannot divorce itself from compassion. If revolt is the right action of the mind, compassion is the adequate move of the heart.

96

When the Otherness of the Other bursts upon the Self, the Self becomes what we can call "compassion-intoxicated." Once the Self is compassionate towards the Other, compassion can change its mode of thinking the world. In other words, compassion is the recognition of the sacredness of the living being. Without compassion, interconnectedness becomes egoism and pride. This is what Lao Tzu calls "the virtue of non-contention." The *Tao Te Ching* argues: "If you protect yourself with compassion you will be impervious."

97

The "virtue of non-contention" leads to the spirit of non-conquest. Conquest has always an aggressive quality: it dominates the Other and hence creates an opposition to itself. Unlike what many people continue to think after five thousand years of human history, conquest does not bring us anything that we do not yet have. It is, therefore, a meaningless action. On the contrary, compassion gains the trust, friendship, and partnership of the Other. There is a beautiful quote by Mandela which says: "If you want to make peace with your enemy, you have to work with your enemy. Then he becomes your partner."

98

The two predominant principles in the modern project of sovereignty and techno-science are "*conquest*" and "*domination*." Descartes develops the idea of domination of Mother Earth by modern civilization with the promise of mastery and possession of Nature by modern science. On the other hand, the Spanish colonization of the Americas is the true expression of a double conquest: that of Nature by modern reason and that of Native Americans by the Conquistadors. Bartolomé de Las Casas and Francisco de Vitoria addressed the fundamental moral and legal questions raised when Europe invaded America. Las Casas opposed the idea supported by Sepulveda and many other Spanish scholars of the time that the Indians were in fact such brutal beings that war against them was morally just. The great battle of compassion was fought by Las Casas against Sepulveda at Valladolid in 1550–1551.

99

> We have no reason to be surprised at the defects, at the uncivilized and excessive customs which we may encounter among the Indian nations, nor to despise them for this. For most if not all the nations of the world have been even more perverted, irrational and depraved, and shown even less caution and wisdom in their manner of government and in their exercise of moral virtues. We ourselves have been much worse in the times of our ancestors and in the length and breadth of our span, as much by the excess and the confusion of manners as by our vices and bestial customs.

These phrases, written by fray Bartolomé de Las Casas in his book *Apologetica Historia*, reflect that the Spanish discovery and subsequent conquest of the New World inspired a serious, if not heated, intellectual controversy regarding the necessity of compassion and humaneness in regard to the Indians.

100

The controversy of Valladolid inaugurated a new debate on the concept of "civilization." Aristotle had already differentiated between human groups, namely the civilized and the barbarians. For Aristotle, the latter were naturally subservient to the former, because for them passion prevailed over reason. Sepúlveda applied this theory to the Indians. According to him, the Indians were a barbarian race whose natural, inferior condition entitled the Spaniards to wage war on them. On the contrary, Las Casas came to conclude that since the Indians were civilized human beings, Spaniards had no right to subject them neither to slavery nor to war. The Las Casas–Sepúlveda controversy was a debate about compassion towards the Otherness of the Other. This debate continues to be of a high significance for us in the 21st century. Its legacy lies in the idea of understanding and addressing the conditions of the "Other" from the Other's perspective.

101

Once, when asked what he thought of Western civilization, Mahatma Gandhi replied, "I think it would be a good idea." By that he meant that humanity was still in the process of civilizing itself by taming its structural violence. In truth, civilization is a potentiality which owes its realization to the coexistence and cooperation of all cultures and traditions of thought. But human civilization is a journey, not a destination. Therefore, it is an unfinished project. We are deluding ourselves if we claim that we have arrived at an achieved civilization.

102

Let us not forget that the price for a civilizing process is neither a strategy of fear nor a politics of hatred. It is a culture of moderation and compassion, the same that Las Casas formulated in his *Apologetica Historia* in the following terms:

> It clearly appears that there are no races in the world, however rude, uncultivated, barbarous, gross, or almost brutal they may be, who cannot be persuaded . . . provided . . . the method that is proper and natural to men is used; that is, love and gentleness and kindness.

It is almost impossible to bear the torch of wisdom and maturity through different cultures of the world without accepting the fact that they can always learn from each other the lessons of life and civilization.

103

The human tendency to regard power and wealth as important has produced very many mediocrities. The noble ideas in the works of human spirits are too often forgotten and dismissed by the shallowness and short-sightedness of our contemporaries who believe in fame more than depth of mind. In today's world, the social position of an intellectual has become infinitely more valuable than the work of the intellect itself. The intellectuals publish books not to enlighten the crowds but to be admired by them. In that sense, thinking is turned into a joke. In an age of celebrities, the crowds would applaud a man or a woman with a Nobel prize but not necessarily an individual with new ideas.

6   The Silence of Wisdom

104

An individual is not born to follow and serve the crowds. The beautiful formation of a human being is not that of being known to everyone but to understand its Zeitgeist in the larger context of eternity. And so, maybe, it will have something new to bring forth to humanity without asking in return for any compliments. No wonder why Kierkegaard believes that, "the humorous self-sufficiency of genius is the unity of a modest resignation in the world and a proud elevation above the world: of being an unnecessary superfluity and a precious ornament." It is certainly true that those who do not live for the approval of the masses can think much easier the world without worrying whether anyone is listening to them. An original work is always accomplished in silence.

105

One is rarely compassionate about oneself. Compassion is a sense of empathy for the Otherness of the Other. There is a huge difference between compassion and pity. In pity, one denies the capabilities of the Other. In compassion, one affirms and participates in the potentials of the Other. The Otherness of the Other is what represents its capabilities and potentialities. The Otherness of a bird is to fly in the sky and that of a fish is to swim in the river or in the ocean. By polluting the skies and destroying the oceans, we disrespect and destroy the "*birdness*" of the birds and the "*fishness*" of the fish. And what about the human beings? What is the Otherness of the humans? It's independence.

106

Independence is a privilege of those who can think for themselves with-out being slaves or flatterers. Independence doesn't mean anything if it is used as an attribute of wealth, power, and violence. One is not independent

DOI: 10.4324/9781003292777-7

because he or she dominates others. Independence is a quality which comes with balance and harmony between the mind and the body. We can talk about independence only when the body and the mind merge to create a perfect harmony. Here we need to revive the traditional concepts which are used in all the martial arts of East Asian origin. It is, therefore, not strange that the philosophy of Zen had much to do with the art of swordsmanship in Japan. According to D.T. Suzuki, "A great fencing master of the Tokugawa period was Miyamoto Musashi (1582–1645), who was the founder of the school called Nitoryu . . ." One of his famous sayings on fencing is: "Under the sword lifted high/There is hell making you tremble;/But go ahead,/And you have the land of bliss."

107

The Japanese art of Zen and the balance between the mind and the body are perhaps more noticeable in the writings and action of a contemporary author like Yukio Mishima. In his book, *Sun and Steel*, Mishima describes the aesthetic value of the body with a reference to the Greek concept of beauty. He argued,

> The theme of estrangement of body and spirit, born of the craving I have described, persisted for a long time as a principal theme in my work. I only came to take gradual leave of it when I at last began to consider whether it was not possible that the body, too, might have its own logic, possibly even its own thought; when I began to feel that the body's special qualities did not lie solely in taciturnity and beauty of form, but that the body too might have its own loquacity.

108

The reality that Mishima tried to convey through a symbiosis between the world of creation and the world of action was that of a struggle within him between the pen and the sword. This was certainly a painful experience for him, like all struggles that hurt. Life is, after all, a permanent struggle which hurts. However, as Suzuki affirms correctly,

> The more you suffer the deeper grows your character, and with the deepening of your character you read the more penetratingly into the secrets of life. All great artists, all great religious leaders, and all great social reformers have come out of the intensest struggles which they fought bravely, quite frequently in tears and with bleeding hearts. Unless you eat your bread in sorrow, you cannot taste of real life.

This "taste of real life" that Suzuki is talking about is the discovery of the Other.

109

It is by confronting the Other that we grow out of our ego-shell. It is the awakening of a self-consciousness confronting another self-consciousness. In Hegelians terms, we can say that a self-consciousness exists *an sich und fur sich* (in itself and for itself), as much as it exists *an sich und fur sich* for the Other. For Hegel, this recognition of Self in the Other ends up in a life-and-death struggle, not an act of compassion. This is because from Hegel's point of view the discipline of mastery and obedience are essential characteristics of self-consciousness. But can a self-consciousness be indifferent to the master–slave distinction? From Hegel's point of view, this has been possible in the Stoic philosophy of "inward freedom" considered by an emperor like Marcus Aurelius and a slave like Epictetus.

110

Though Hegel considered the Stoic freedom as an empty and abstract freedom drawn away from objective life, it would be interesting to get a glimpse into the Stoic philosophy in relation with the problematic of the Otherness of the Other. It is well known that a philosopher like Seneca considered his duty to be kind and forgiving to the Other. He explains this opinion in his *Letter XLVIII to Lucilius*: "No one can lead a happy life if he thinks only of himself and turns everything to his own purposes. You should live for the other person if you wish to live for yourself." The Stoics believed in the existence of a common moral principle for all mankind. As such, they saw the world as a community of friends and brothers ruled by the divine will and the laws of nature. Unsurprisingly, wisdom, courage, and justice were the key concepts used in Stoic philosophy.

111

In Book Nine of his *Meditations*, Marcus Aurelius writes:

> Whoever commits injustice acts irreverently; for since universal nature has created rational creatures for the sake of one another, to benefit their fellows according to their deserts and in no way to do them harm, it is plain that one who offends against her will is guilty of irreverence towards the most venerable of gods.

What Marcus Aurelius is pointing out here is getting to the ethical nutshell of Stoic philosophy, which points out that one's happiness depends on that of all others. Thus, one needs to act virtuously in order to benefit other human beings.

> For nothing is as effective in creating greatness of mind as being able to examine methodically and truthfully everything that presents itself in life, and always viewing things in such a way as to consider what kind of use each thing serves in what kind of a universe. And what value it has to human beings as citizens of that highest cities of which all other cities are, as it were, mere households.

112

Stoic philosophers made reference to virtues such as courage, simplicity, and self-sufficiency. It is interesting that we find the same virtues more than eighteen centuries later in the Gandhian doctrine of nonviolence. For Gandhi, nonviolence has a spiritual content which goes in the direction of the Gandhian ideas of simplicity and self-sufficiency as experiential modes of self-transformation. It goes without saying that for Gandhi self-transformation is a collective capacity to live in harmony. Unsurprisingly, "harmony" is a key concept in Stoic philosophy. As Marcus Aurelius says: "He who lives in harmony with himself lives in harmony with the universe." It would be interesting to make a rapprochement between the concept of "harmony" in Stoicism and the saying of His Holiness the Dalai Lama. According to His Holiness: "Because we all share this planet earth, we have to live in harmony and peace with each other and with Nature. This is not just a dream, but a necessity."

113

In the philosophy of the Otherness of the Other, there is no conquest and domination of Nature. If we consider the "*natureness*" of Nature (what Spinoza calls *natura naturans*: the self-causing activity of Nature), we will learn not to approach it as an amenable instrument for our well-being but as a spiritual entity. "Nature never becomes a toy to a wise spirit," writes Emerson. As such, we are not pure spectators of Nature, but actors who participate *in* and *with* Nature. This is where Zen Buddhism can be of a great help. As Suzuki underlines:

> Zen does not try to disengage us from the world, to make us mere spectators of the hurly-burly which we see around us. Zen is not mysticism, if the latter is to be understood in the sense of escapism. Zen is right in

the midst of the ocean of becoming. It shows no desire to escape from its tossing waves, It does not antagonize Nature; it does not treat Nature as if it were an enemy to be conquered, nor does it stand away from Nature. It is indeed Nature itself.

114

The cosmic companionship of Man and Nature has been a perennial theme among the thinkers of the East and the West. Rabindranath Tagore was among those artists who was in search of a unity between life and art through Nature. For Tagore, Man is in search of the everlasting joy and rhythm in the stream of Nature. Therefore, the invitation is there, always, from the world of Nature to the world of Man. In other words, in Tagore's mind, the vision of Nature is an important component for the renewal of a vision of humanity. Therefore, to sit face to face with Nature is to be blessed with the prized moment of the All Beautiful. "Beauty," writes Tagore in his book *Creative Unity*, "is that profound expression of reality which satisfies our hearts without any other allurements but its own ultimate value." Tagore considers the aesthetic experience of Nature as a joy of empathy, which consists of being lifted out of the Self and being identified with the objects of Nature. However, according to Tagore, this aesthetic experience is not only an *outwardization* of the Self but also an *inwardization* of objects.

115

An interesting point in Tagore's philosophy of Otherness is that his vision of Nature serves as a basis for his vision of social awareness. According to Tagore, the efflorescence of social awareness is the outcome of the inner being that fully endorses the cause of well-being of each and every natural being near and far. This vision of Nature is accomplished in Tagore's thought by a non-static idea of culture. In other words, Tagore's belief in a world with multiple voices advocates cultural fusions between East and West and encourages an overriding commitment to universal peace. We can find the same philosophical attitude in both Ralph Waldo Emerson and Henry David Thoreau.

116

"Nature always wears the colors of the spirit," proclaims Emerson. Therefore, to a person with no spiritual eye, Nature is nothing but a landscape which can be urbanized. The "spirit" that Emerson talks about can help us transcend our separation from the Earth. We can find the same ecological understanding of change in Henry David Thoreau. "How meanly and grossly do we deal with nature!" writes Thoreau in 1842. He continues:

> Could we not have a less gross labor? What else do these fine inventions suggest-magnetism, the daguerreotype, electricity? Can we do no more than cut and trim the forest-can we not assist in its interior economy, in the circulation of the sap? Now we work superficially and violently. We do not suspect how much might be done to improve our relation with animated nature; what kindness and refined courtesy there might be.

117

Thoreau contests the reductionist idea of progress, as it has been formulated in the modern paradigm of capitalism and technology. The miracle of growth and accumulation is nothing but the conquest of Nature and human beings by the steam engine and colonial powers. Unlike the indigenous cultures (e.g., the Native Americans and Canadians) who venerated Nature as a sacred element, the reductionist view of political and techno-scientific modernity exercised a patriarchal power over all natural elements which ended in an ecological catastrophe. As a result, affirms Thoreau, "This world is a place for business . . . I think that there is nothing, not even crime, more opposed to poetry, to philosophy, ay, to life itself, than this incessant business."

118

The majestic quality of Thoreau's thinking is not only its critical sense of turning against the tide but also the dissenting quality of his social rebelliousness. As a solitary individual, who finds his sanctuary in Nature (more precisely at the Walden Pond), Thoreau invites us to follow the sunrise and the sunset every day. In his essay, *Life Without Principle*, he writes: "Really to see the sun rise or go down every day, so to relate ourselves to a universal fact, would preserve us sane forever." That is why Thoreau continues to be an inspiration for all those who believe in dissent as a mode of questioning and thinking in contemporary society. It is also undeniable that Thoreau had a great influence on the powerful ideas of Mahatma Gandhi and Martin Luther King, Jr. According to Howard Zinn, "Thoreau's great insight was that there is a moral emptiness in government unless it is filled by the action of citizens on behalf of justice." That is the reason why, Thoreau is trying not only to correct modern Man's relation to Nature but also to re-evaluate and rectify the status of citizens in regards to the laws and institutions in a modern State.

119

Nonviolent democratic theory has seldom presented a better principle than civil disobedience to bring high personal courage next to the struggle for freedom. Accordingly, Thoreau did not consider politics a power-making business and he did not want his contemporaries to be kept contended by cheap politics. And so since he didn't take any pleasure of modern politics, he decided to refine it with ethics. It is through his essay on disobedience that Thoreau entered into the general consciousness of humanity.

120

It is through his appeal to disobedience of unjust laws that Thoreau permanently affected men and women's fundamental convictions to fight for justice. For Thoreau, disobedience is a political urge toward a moral perfection. In other words, disobedience is a path to balance and maturity, not a road to social chaos. Like Socrates, Thoreau was concerned about life as an examined process. He repeated Socrates' "The unexamined life is not worth living" in his own words: "Let us consider the way in which we spend our lives." By saying this, Thoreau wanted to defeat the conformism and complacency of his time. Thoreau always considered it a duty to disobey unjust laws. He firmly believed that every citizen is ultimately responsible for every act of the state. Henry David Thoreau starts his essay on *Civil Disobedience* with the motto "That government is best which governs least" and continues by saying "That government is best which governs not at all." Actually, Thoreau's philosophy of revolt in this essay is a meaningful opposition to the meaningless complexities of modern civilization. More than half a century later, Gandhi formulated the same criticism under the spell of Tolstoy, Thoreau, and Ruskin in his seminal work *Hind Swaraj*.

7　An Examined Civilization

121

Hind Swaraj is the strongest non-Western criticism ever addressed to modern civilization. For Gandhi, writing *Hind Swaraj* was not just a political act against British colonialism but also a call upon the people of the world, including the Westerners, to think and work towards a better future, that is based upon the welfare of all around the planet. To be more exact *Hind Swaraj* could be read and understood as a manifesto for the Otherness of the Other. For Gandhi, modern civilization is based on a flawed view and it suffers from several basic and interrelated limitations: It lacks moral and spiritual depth and creates violence.

122

Gandhi introduces his readers to a new model of civilization which takes humanity to a higher moral level. While pointing to the fallacy of utilitarianism as a false mode of existence which dismisses totally the welfare of the Other, Gandhi suggests his own idea of "*Swaraj*" as a self-rule and self-realization which can develop in a habit of shared sovereignty and empathetic pluralism. For Gandhi, civilization has to give primacy to moral progress of humanity. Therefore, his measuring instrument for moral progress of the human race is interdependence. Gandhi is not against human development in history, but for him there is no growth without harmonic exchange. This means that there is no such thing as a welfare for all, if citizens of the planet do not temper their greed and ambitions through moral law. In one word, Gandhi believes that civilization should help humanity realize the path of righteousness and compassion, by putting morality before materialism.

DOI: 10.4324/9781003292777-8

123

According to Gandhi, civilization should help humanity reach the *telos* of self-realization. That is why Gandhi redefines civilization as a mode of conduct, which points out to human beings the path of nonviolence. For Gandhi, nonviolence is the path of duty which secures the rights of individuals. But we should understand that our moral progress is first and foremost towards self-realization and love force. It is only through this path that we can respect both the human dignity and the Otherness of the Other. In his quest to defend self-realization, Gandhi challenges both the individual and institutional harms and evils. He invites individuals to rule themselves against their weaker natures by becoming self-governing agents. But he also looks for the creation and cultivation of a public culture of citizenship that guarantees to everyone the right to opinion and action, as an alternative to state structures.

124

For Gandhi, violence was a sign of the failure of a legitimate political power. At the core of Gandhi's political theory is the view of politics as shaped by internal moral power, rather than from the standpoint of rational violence. Consequently, for Gandhi, the modern state contained forces that threatened, rather than enhanced, liberty. Therefore, he did not consider democracy as a political regime but as a value, which needed to be created and cherished. His defence of institutions of the liberal constitutional state did not mean that he justified them in terms of his political philosophy. To the contrary, politics for Gandhi was an act of consciousness, not a mode of living taken for granted. Gandhi did not see the goal of political action as the immediate capture of office. According to him, the basic condition of political action was the elimination of violence. His principal aim was to civilize modern politics from within, by shorting the circuit of resentment, hatred, and coercion. His politics of nonviolence was a method to mobilize collective power in a manner that attends to its own moral education in an exemplary and innovative way. Gandhi showed that a life of excellence is an agency and a transformative force, an experience of conscience underpinning the harmony between ethics and politics.

125

The Gandhian appeal to the ethical in politics was not only a way to seek Truth but also of coming to know oneself in ever-greater depth. The

Gandhian effort for nonviolent politics was a cultivation of one's capacity for ethical citizenship. That is to say, Gandhi considered politics as a work of the heart and not merely of reason. This recalls French philosopher Blaise Pascal, who said: "The heart has its reasons which reason itself does not know." In the same manner, Gandhi believed that the heart, and not reason, is the seat of morality. He wrote "Morality which depends upon the helplessness of a man or woman has not much to recommend it. Morality is rooted in the purity of our hearts." Gandhi believed that next to constructive work, a society also needs to be inwardly empowered, since human beings are capable of love, compassion, solidarity, and empathy. From Gandhi's perspective, nonviolence was an ontological truth that followed from the unity and interdependence of humanity and life. Therefore, he advocated an awareness of the essential unity of humanity. That awareness called for critical self-examination and a move from egocentricity towards a "shared humanity."

126

Let us think closely about this "shared humanity." This "shared humanity" cannot exist if it is not aware of its shortcomings. It needs to strive to remove its ethical imperfections in order to be able to live with global challenges. We are living in an age of increasing "globalization of selfishness," so there is an urgent need to understand the Otherness of the Other, starting with the natural environment surrounding us and ending with the domain of politics and economics. Understanding the Otherness of the Other is to break the so-called cycle of barbarity. Maybe what perplexes individuals so much about the concept of the Otherness of the Other is that it is seen and felt as a newcomer in our lives. Yet Otherness of the Other is the common horizon of humanity, because it includes the Self and the Other. Unlike exclusion, hatred, and violence, the Otherness of the Other is not an automatic response to a crisis. It is much more reflective. All human beings can be reflective, in the sense in which thinking about what one does is part of doing it. So why do we have difficulty thinking about Otherness of the Other?

127

The Self has nobility and dignity only to the extent which it tries to understand the Other and have empathy for its existence. We are all children of a double heritage, a mixture of horror of exclusion and murder on the one hand with courage and beauty on the other hand, as modes of living and sharing. Camus said, "We live in terror because persuasion is no longer possible; because man has been wholly submerged in history." But sometimes we need to stop the train of history and get off, maybe because we need to think and write about the presence of the evil in the world, in order to survive. In other words, to talk like Dostoevsky, we must coexist and maintain a shared level of responsibility, because we are all responsible to one another.

128

There is no way for us to understand and practise empathy and interconnectedness with the Otherness of the Other if we refuse to acknowledge the need of humanity for beauty and compassion, for an aesthetic sense of life. Truly, it is in this common potential for compassion and beauty that we can find the fruits of recognition and reconciliation. But, let us also not forget that tyrants have always feared beauty, maybe because beauty represents the voice of the Otherness of the Other. Even today, our world tries to make beauty insignificant, but creating beauty is the most passionate way of expressing life. Roland Barthes says, "To see someone who does not see is the best way to be intensely aware of what he does not see." The beauty seekers are those who try to see what the people don't see and to turn it into what is visible. In today's world, those who create beauty are tightrope walkers, because the war against beauty is always waged in the language of utility and functionalism.

129

Beauty is an idea which is unappreciated and taken for granted in today's world. But, actually in an ugly human world as ours, beauty is something we should fight for. It is not a gift which is offered to us on a golden plate. However, very often we forget that we need beauty as we need oxygen and we should fight for it every second, every minute, and every hour of the day. Yet, creating beauty, while listening to the Otherness of the Other, is not a virtue of our de-civilizing world. Only a truly ethico-aesthetic approach which listens to the Other with empathy and compassion, which learns from the horrors of the past, can reverse the meaninglessness and thoughtlessness of the de-civilizing process we are currently going through and create a true cosmic companionship. Now, the powerful question is: Is there a limit on how much empathy and companionship we are capable of toward the Other?

130

As we saw previously, full understanding of the process of freedom-making necessitates a civilizational acceptance of the Other as the Other. Empathy (what Herder called *Einfuhlung*) plays an important role in this process.

It is sharing with another person or another culture its great achievements and its sufferings. However, we live a crisis of "empathy" in today's world. The question of "utility" which has replaced the idea of "empathy" is the regulating idea in today's world. It is, therefore, imperative that members of different cultures engage in critical intercultural dialogue whereby they try to understand each other before indulging in the criticism of cultural practices which they find offensive. As Kant puts it, engaging and diverse viewpoints enrich and inform our political modes of relating with others, as without plurality of "being with others" we cannot liberate our mind from [the] darkness of ignorance. However, individuality cannot be realized without the ability "to analyze and think for self."

131

Most, if not all, living civilizations change and evolve over time. No civilization constitutes a hermetically sealed ensemble. The boundaries of a civilization may change as it encounters other civilizations. This is actually how it has been all through human history. In that case, critical inter-civilizational dialogue could lead to change where the process of dialogue and transvaluation of values replaces that of coercion and manipulation. When it is done in this manner, the partners in an inter-civilizational dialogue end up engaging in a process of questioning rather than intimidating or patronizing each other.

132

Today, unfortunately, we are closer to a one-dimensional idea of civilization, expressed in de-civilizing terms, rather than to a genuine inter-civilizational humanity with a shared understanding. As such, what is shared is more the time which is spent for chatting on social media than an understanding of world culture. As a result, people around the world know more about what is on sold at Amazon or eBay, rather than what is the difference between the author of *Divine Comedy* and that of *Brothers Karamazov*. Some cynical spirits might return the argument by saying that even in the past only elites knew about these things. This might be the case, but never in the memory of humankind, humanity has been so informed and so stupid at the same time. The best example for this is what we can observe in the domain of politics.

133

Politics has become meaningless in today's world: both on the side of the leaders and the citizens. The desire to turn citizens into unquestioning, unaccountable, and servile human beings has become the principal motive for the development of politics in the contemporary world. The rise of populist politicians around the world is harbinger of a worrying trend: zombified populations are marching to the order of big mouth demagogues, with little respect to or comprehension of the political process and practice. However, the rise of the demagogues is the symptom, not the cause of erosion of public trust and engagement. Therefore, divisive politics that pushes citizens into small bubbles and preaches nativism contributes to the decline of citizenry.

134

The language of exclusion has become very present in our world. It might not show itself anymore in hard ideological language, but it certainly appears in the liberal fetishization of legality. This is when justice is no longer about compassion but only a table of abstract regulations that people use or abuse without care for the other person. The truth is that, especially in the liberal countries, we are not equipped for the truth anymore. It is said that "all men are born equal" but that is not true. Those who suffer from poverty, violence, malnutrition, and illiteracy are not born into equal circumstances. But we see them and read about them as temporary subjects, accidents of our glorious human civilization. The liberal language of exclusion easily lends itself to the invention of a barbarian world.

135

Most of the barbarities in the world are sustained in the name of a reductionist view of civilization and humanity. Here we have the total absence of the empathetic listening of the Other. But we should never forget what Arendt writes on this subject, and this is central to our debate on revenge and forgiveness: "If it were true that sovereignty and freedom are the same, then indeed no man could be free, because sovereignty, the ideal of uncompromising self-sufficiency and mastership, is contradictory to the very condition of plurality." Moreover, pluralism implies a community of human beings who are listening and can be listened to. The possibility of speech and that of listening are modes of emphasizing on the Otherness of the Other against all forms of barbarity.

136

The key question would be: should one be tolerant in regard to barbarity? Consequently, barbarity is the Otherness of the barbarian (the Other). But who is the barbarian? For the ancient Greeks, the barbarian was the person who replaced the real human language with mumbling. The Romans would also oppose *feritas*, (bestiality) to *humanitas*. We see that in both cases, the barbarian is the Other relegated to a geographical, cultural, or linguistic distance. In modern times, with the rise of the idea of "progress," the barbarian would become the underdeveloped. This Manichean conception of reality has been predominant until today. However, anthropologists like Levi-Strauss have tried to define "barbarity" in a different way. According to Levi-Strauss, "The barbarian is first of all the human being who believes in barbarity." In other words, it would be more correct to talk about the barbarian not as the Other (as the Greeks and Romans did) but as the "cruel Self."

137

We can define barbarity as inhumanity and cruelty. But what is cruelty? In the eyes of Montaigne, "All that is beyond simple death seems to [be] pure cruelty." In other words, cruelty is an act that arouses horror. The difference between the Holocaust and a simple murder is that the latter is an act of barbarity. Nazis were not everyday ordinary Germans. They were barbarians. Barbarity was the Otherness of the Nazis. Schiller in his *Letters on the Aesthetic Education of Man* (*Über die ästhetische Erziehung des Menschen in einer Reihe von Briefen)* asks the following question: how is it, then, that we still remain barbarians? Schiller considers reason as an ethically insufficient faculty.

138

From Schiller's point of view, we need a sensuous responsiveness to the Other. Now, regardless of whether or not Schiller himself practised this "sensuous responsiveness," it goes without saying that his aesthetic dimension of ethics can be used as a project of empathy for the Otherness of the Other. If barbarity is the enemy of empathy, then the project of caring for the Otherness of the Other would suggest a mode of sensibility that rejects the logic of conquest of Man and the World. To speak like the late French philosopher, Michel Henry, barbarity has a negating power of life and of any value other than itself (this is how Henry characterizes modern science). As a result, says Henry, "the culture is rejected in the clandestine situation of an underground." This is where we stand today: menaced by a new barbarity, that of techno-science and mass communication, which puts into question 50 centuries of human culture by publicizing and educating mediocrity and banality.

139

Nietzsche was well aware of the barbarity of modern times, when he wrote in *Beyond Good and Evil*: "Like the rider on a steed snorting to go further onward, we let the reins drop before the infinite, we modern men, we half-barbarians – and we feel supremely happy only when we are in the most – *danger*." Nietzsche knew well that the future of humanity has tied a knot with a new barbarity. Not long ago, this barbarity manifested itself at Auschwitz, Gulag, Hiroshima, and many other places on the planet Earth. But whenever and wherever humanity has short memory, barbarity manifests itself with a new face and in a new appearance. The new Hiroshima of 21st century is not nuclear, it is ecological.

8   The Nobility of Spirit

140

One of the virtues of today's humanity is to hide its face from all the mirrors. Maybe because, it is difficult for modernity to admit that by fighting barbarity it has turned itself into a new barbarian. As Nietzsche notifies us: "Whoever fights monsters should see to it that in the process he does not become a monster. And when you look long into an abyss, the abyss also looks into you." Truly, we have looked long into the abyss of meaninglessness and mediocrity. Now, mediocrity is looking back at us and is asking us to follow it. We are best punished for our modern dreams.

141

Not all modern dreams have ended in barbarity and the negation of the Otherness of the Other. Let us take for example Beethoven's *Fidelio*. *Fidelio* occupies a special place in the pantheon of Beethoven's great works. Singular though it may be, *Fidelio* reveals the full measure of Beethoven's Zeitgeist and his humanistic idealism. Maybe that is why Beethoven's *Fidelio* exemplifies the depth of the artist's spiritual nature and the excellence of his lived experience. We can take Beethoven's *Fidelio* not only as an exemplar piece of music but also as a musical expression of moral exemplarity. This means that the ethical message of *Fidelio* can never be completely understood unless the ethical characteristic of Beethoven's aesthetic representation is revealed.

142

Beethoven's *Fidelio* unlike many other musical oeuvres has continuously developed in maturity for different listeners in the past 200 years, because it has been the spiritual expression of an attitude towards life that has within it

DOI: 10.4324/9781003292777-9

the possibility of thinking life beyond suffering. This tale of political idealism, resistance to tyranny, and marital fidelity comes to a climax when the
heroine Leonore prepares to sacrifice her life to protect her imprisoned husband Florestan from the evil Pizarro; the couple is saved at the last minute
by the arrival of the good minister Don Fernando, who has Pizarro arrested.
Therefore, *Fidelio* is a work like no other. It is an opera that allows a listener
to become not only a great passionate of classical music but also a passionate of freedom. *Fidelio* is naturally a revolutionary opera or more precisely
an opera which echoes the ideal of the revolutionary age in music.

143

This opera, like so much of Beethoven's music, can reveal much of its power
Beethoven's "child of sorrow" is an opera of the people, it is a portrayal of
little people doing great things like a woman disguising herself as a man in
order to rescue her political prisoner husband. But, as the characters take on
a more symbolic quality, *Fidelio* goes beyond simple scenery or theatrical
expression and becomes what Wilhelm Furtwängler not long after the end
of World War II called "a Mass." In the words of Furtwängler, *Fidelio* is

> not an opera in the sense we are used to, nor is Beethoven a musician
> for the theatre, or a dramaturge. He is quite a bit more, a whole musi-
> cian, and beyond that, a saint and a visionary. That which disturbs us is
> not a material effect, nor the fact of the "imprisonment"; any film could
> create the same effect. No, it is the music, it is Beethoven himself. It is
> this "nostalgia of liberty" he feels, or better, makes us feel; this is what
> moves us to tears. His *Fidelio* has more of the Mass than of the Opera
> to it; the sentiments it expresses come from the sphere of the sacred, and
> preach a "religion of humanity" which we never found so beautiful or
> necessary as we do today, after all we have lived through. Herein lies
> the singular power of this unique opera. . . . Independent of any histori-
> cal consideration . . . the flaming message of Fidelio touches deeply.
> We realize that for we Europeans, as for all men, this music will always
> represent an appeal to our conscience.

144

Wilhelm Furtwängler makes reference to *Fidelio* in order to explain how
much the opera meant to those who survived the trauma of World War II. Is
it any coincidence, then, that in December of 1944, as the Battle of the Bulge
was taking place in Europe, Toscanini conducted a two-part radio broadcast
of Beethoven's *Fidelio* and made it clear that "Beethoven believed in liberty

and was opposed to tyrants such as Napoleon Bonaparte and would have likely opposed Adolf Hitler and Benito Mussolini as well." As such, with its message of liberty, *Fidelio*, whether on the stage or in the pit, stands musically against all forms of tyranny. *Fidelio* is not a work about the characters, at least not primarily. It is about an idea, certainly the most glorious idea of all: freedom.

145

Because ethical and musical values intertwine so closely in Beethoven's music, their priority must remain a matter of personal inclination. For some listeners, the political thought in Beethoven's music matters chiefly as it illuminates the expressive force of his musical thought. After Beethoven, it was impossible to consider music only as beautiful sounds, as was the music of Mozart. Beethoven transformed it from a mere form to a powerful and at the same time intimate expression of his innermost feelings. It is true that we are accustomed to the conjunction of Mozart and Beethoven. The reasons are obvious. Beethoven and Mozart were the two most important and influential musicians of their time. And yet, as Adorno once suggested, the fourteen years which separate the births of the two composers is deeply marked by the French Revolution and its concomitant transformation of Enlightenment political ideas. Curiously enough, Beethoven's *Fidelio* is the only opera from the first decade of the 19th century which depicts the new republican spirit of the French Revolution. In words of Edward Said,

> *Fidelio* is in many ways not only Beethoven's remorselessly middle-class answer to Mozart's libertine perspectives in the Da Ponte operas but also an attempt to give musical life to a set of abstract ideas about human justice and freedom taken from the French Revolution.

Fidelio is an opera that not only contrasts patriotic heroism and individualistic self-interest but also underlines the virtuous life of a republican community.

146

Let us say simply and clearly that Beethoven's *Fidelio* is one of the greatest expressions of Otherness of the Other in history of music. That is to say, in *Fidelio*, Beethoven's music proves itself to be the aesthetic representation of the timeless resistance against the inhumane. As such, Beethoven reaches in *Fidelio* a state of consciousness that only the great spirits of nonviolence like Buddha, St. Francis, and Gandhi ever reached, meaning where there are no boundaries between the Self and the Other. It is, therefore, because of this experience of the Otherness of the Other, that Beethoven's *Fidelio* has lived as a permanent aesthetic and ethical value to our human race. Generally speaking, listening to a certain type of music, like *Fidelio*, could be a defiant act in situation of tyranny.

147

One thing that no tyranny can tolerate is the Otherness of the Other. Simply because, for tyrannies and tyrants, there is no such thing as the Other. To speak like George Orwell in *Nineteen Eighty-Four*, Otherness is not statistical. That is why a 20th-century composer like Olivier Messiaen could say that: "birds are the greatest musicians existing on our planet." Messiaen communicated with the "birdness" of the birds through his new musical language, in the same way as St. Francis of Assisi did it through spirituality. There is a legendary tale about St. Francis and the birds which have been repeated by his biographers:

> Saint Francis lifted up his eyes, and saw on some trees by the wayside a great multitude of birds . . . and the substance of the sermon [to them] was this: "My little sisters the birds, ye owe much to God, your Creator, and ye ought to sing his praise at all times and in all places, because he has given you liberty to fly about into all places; and though ye neither spin nor sew, he has given you a twofold and a threefold clothing for yourselves and for your offspring; besides which, he feeds you, though ye neither sow nor reap. He has given you fountains and rivers to quench your thirst, mountains, and valleys in which to take refuge, and trees in which to build your nests; so that your Creator loves you much, having thus favoured you with such bounties. Beware, my little sisters, of the sin of ingratitude, and study always to give praise to God." As he said these words, all the birds began to open their beaks, to stretch their necks, to spread their wings, and reverently to bow their heads to the ground, endeavouring by their motions and by their songs to manifest their joy to Saint Francis. And the saint rejoiced with them.

This legendary tale of the birds represents act 2, scene 6 of Olivier Messiaen's opera *Saint Francis*. Messiaen himself was free like a bird, not only in the way he approached the birdness of the birds but also in his appreciation of the world of music. He proclaimed in 1972: "I don't belong to any kind of school; I'm neither a follower of serial music, nor am I a composer of a 'new sound,' nor do I champion the cause of any special modes."

148

Such an attitude not only makes possible marginality of Being but also introduces us to a plurality of vision. Consequently, a creator who is in search of the Otherness of the Other needs to be an outsider in order to develop its critical capacities against all forms of conformism. The pattern that sets the course for a creator as an outsider is best exemplified by the condition of a dissenter, who never fully feels at home with any question. Dissent for the creator in search of the Otherness of the Other is a constant sense of being unsettled. The creator's role is, therefore, to present the Otherness of the Other as an alternative narrative against grand narratives of the Self.

149

The creator-dissenter has the capacity to break out of the mental ghettos since it is guided by a permanent metaphysical homelessness. This continuous practice of questioning presents itself as a form of resistance to the "sameness" of reality. This is an opportunity in the domain of creativity to express the universality of the human experience through an increased cross-cultural understanding, ultimately fostering harmony and reducing conflict among human beings. But the same attitude of empathy could exist to the biodiversity of the non-human world. We should not forget that Mother Earth is the place where we get a common identity as living beings. Diversity is, therefore, not only diversity of cultures, religions, traditions, and nations, but it is also the diversity of life.

150

A genuine creator-dissenter is someone who heeds humanness while at the same time subjecting it to merciless scrutiny. Therefore, we should understand that our humanness is burdened with an enormous responsibility. There is a special responsibility of humanity to address its instituted powers of one's own rationality, which are accountable to life on Earth, particularly because those powers are exercised in a manifestly disproportionate and barbaric manner against all that is non-human. That is to say, diversity becomes a very important pre-condition when thinking in terms of the Otherness of the Other. We can define diversity here not only as a form of multi-dimensionality but also as empathetic understanding and compassionate interconnectedness.

151

We should focus on the essence of life itself. Thoreau suggested the following: "Live in each season as it passes; breathe the air, drink the drink, taste the fruit, and resign yourself to the influence of the earth." In other words, we need to look at the Otherness of life as a sacred thing. For a desacralized market economy, a cow is considered as wrapped meat in supermarkets. When we destroy the "*cowness*" of the cows, we can send them with a cold moral indifference to the slaughterhouse. There is only one step from the slaughterhouse to the Nazi gas chambers. The same cruelty and spirit of murder that lives in a slaughterhouse can become that of a Nazi concentration camp. As Adorno says: "Auschwitz begins whenever someone looks at a slaughterhouse and thinks: they're only animals." History has shown us that human beings are capable of killing all living creatures, including individuals from their own species.

152

Our differences with the plant and animal kingdoms should not prevail over our shared world. The world is not only ours, but it also belongs to all living beings. As such, the bell of any cruelty against plants and animals does not toll for any one tree or cow. It also tolls for humanity, which at every step of cruelty against life, approaches the moment of Last Judgement for itself. When we say that life is sacred, we mean that life cannot be on a billboard. The true lesson of Auschwitz is not only about the evil of Nazism and anti-Semitism but also about the sacredness of life. At the ontological level, the exclusion of the Otherness of the Other implies a mutilated life.

9   Empathy and Conquest

153

"Freedom," Winston Smith argues in George Orwell's memorable novel, *Nineteen Eighty-Four*, "is the freedom to say that two plus two make four." But what if two plus two make five. What then? Maybe we should take off the techno-scientific blindfold and look at life as it flows. The epistemological arrogance of market fundamentalism is a great threat to the future of life on Earth. So if we want to proceed with an ecology of transformation, we need to liberate our minds from the reductionist logic of a mechanistic science which is unable to see beyond the machine. The fear that this reductionist logic creates in the hearts and minds of the poor and peasants around the world is intensified by corporate cannibals which have no sense of biodiversity. In corporate cannibalism, the conquest of the Earth goes hand in hand with the conquest of human beings.

154

The philosophy of the Otherness of the Other is based on the idea of plurality of knowledge. What the corporate mindset suggests to us at the level of financial, political, or even academic institutions is that the end of knowledge is success. This corporate dream of success, which starts in Silicon Valley and ends in Shanghai and Mumbai, is a one-dimensional view of Man and Nature. In such a paradigm, everything is raw material for market economy and techno-capitalist domination of the Earth. In such a case, every bit of life on the planet is quantifiable and should enter the utilitarian logic of global production and quality control. As a result, the conquest of the Earth by global corporations is the end of decentralized and democratic organization of life, but at the same time, it destroys the traditional forms of knowledge that populations around the world have learned and practised for centuries as an art of living. In today's world, the art of living of peasants,

DOI: 10.4324/9781003292777-10

tribes, nomads, and indigenous people are misunderstood, dismissed, and discarded by the global market and governments around the world. We can take here the example of Canada, a country where formal apologies were expressed by the government for the past cruelties of the White Canadians against the First Nations. But this gesture of apology is immediately accompanied by a total indifference to the inherent right of the First Nations to self-determination and self-government.

155

The 1910 *History of Canada* text book for Ontario Public Schools taught young Canadians that:

> All Indians were superstitious, having strange ideas about nature. They thought that birds, beasts . . . were like men. Thus an Indian has been known to make a long speech of apology to a wounded bear. Such were the people whom the pioneers of our own race found lording it over the North American continent – this untamed savage of the forest who could not bring himself to submit to the restraints of European life.

This quote is very often completed by that of a racist Canadian civil servant by the name of Duncan Campbell Scott, involved in Aboriginal affairs, who is famous for having said:

> I want to get rid of the Indian problem. I do not think as a matter of fact, that the country ought to continuously protect a class of people who are able to stand alone. . . . Our objective is to continue until there is not a single Indian in Canada that has not been absorbed into the body politic and there is no Indian question, and no Indian Department, that is the whole object of this Bill.

This is a great example of the spirit of conquest and genocide practised by the modern civilization in the name of a mono-cultural rationality. For those who have not lost their capacity of looking and thinking critically, a politically correct cultural genocide has become the true face of globalization.

156

There is always a way in which, irrespective of the catastrophic circumstances which have totally disseminated languages, cultures, and living creatures from the surface of the planet Earth, a philosophy of the Otherness of the Other would provide us with a new challenge to address. Though the future of humanity is very uncertain and dark when it comes to the ecological destruction of the natural environment and indigenous cultures, a step forward in the direction of epistemic humility might function as a small lamp which might be able to light future lamps. Such a perspective cannot take place without humanity transcending the narrow corporate identity that we experiment around us. Moreover, humanity can change in the right direction, by saving itself and the world, but it needs to live differently and think differently. No matter, what history shows us, compassion and empathy can change the world.

157

Nothing great was ever achieved without empathy. The empathetic way of life is wonderful, because it is compassionate to the Otherness of the Other. There is no compassion which is final; all compassions are initial. There is a time in every human being's life when he/she arrives at the conviction that one cannot advance alone in the Dark. And therefore, each one of us should know how to esteem and respect the Otherness of the Other. However, we can never attain this level of consciousness with conformity and complacency. And that is why Emerson proclaims: "For non-conformity the world whips you with its displeasure." But the displeasure of the crowd is always the virtue of an individual who knows how to keep its head above shallowness and mediocrity. One can be empathetic and compassionate while being an outsider. Nothing can bring us balance and harmony but an empathetic outsiderhood.

158

Life is profoundly guided by this sense of outsiderhood. Most of the greatest insights in human history result from the advantage of being an outsider. Actually, outsiderhood is the great quality of great characters. As Baltasar Gracian underlines in *The Pocket Oracle and Art of Prudence*, "a single quality is the equivalent of many mediocre ones." This said, outsiderhood is mainly a condition of profound creative empowerment. But there is also a more interesting dimension of never feeling fully at home in a fixed solid entity. The nomadic essence of outsiderhood which is expressed in a creative mode of being is also a condition to call the values and institutions of society to account and examine their level of changeability. In general, one may say that the foundations of outsiderhood are not in the institutions but in the nobility of spirit.

159

All human beings are in some degree impressed by the nobility of spirit; however, some are much more than the others. This nobility is neither natural nor social; it is aesthetic. The spirit of an individual is noble because it seeks beauty. Beauty, in its most meaningful sense, is one expression of the Otherness of the Other. If we seek the Otherness of the Other, it is because we search the beautiful. The love of the Otherness of the Other is the love of beauty. But the Otherness of the Other is only so far beautiful as it suggests empathy. This is why empathy is a creative mode of being. Through empathy, we seek each to concentrate the love of beauty on one point: that is, the Otherness of the Other. The world, thus, exists as an expression of beauty in the whole, which is expressed by the artist. Even if the world is like hell, it is still beautiful in the eyes of the artist. As Michelangelo writes in one of his poems: "I live in hell and paint its pictures." It didn't matter to Michelangelo, the creator, to be in hell or in paradise. In both cases, his creations are a challenge to God's creation of the world.

160

As Ananda Coomaraswamy affirms, art is "a wisdom to be applied to everyday matters." That is why Coomaraswamy considers the rise of modern culture as a total "bankruptcy in all aspects of human life." "What we call civilization," wrote Coomaraswamy, "is nothing but a murderous machine without conscience or ideals . . . Civilization is an anomaly, not to say a monstrosity." Coomaraswamy's complete distrust of the modern culture is accompanied by his profound and uncompromising adherence to the concept of "tradition." What interests him is the "traditional" rather than any specific form of tradition. For him, as for the other thinkers of the Perennial School such as Frithjof Schuon and Titus Burckhardt, the "traditional" refers to the central idea that all religions derive from a single primordial transcendental source. In a letter to Alfred O. Mendel, Coomaraswamy explains what he clearly understands by the word "tradition." "'Tradition' has nothing to do with any 'ages,' whether 'dark,' 'primaeval,' or otherwise. Tradition represents doctrines about first principles, which do not change; and traditional institutions represent the application of these principles in particular environments." Admitting Guenon's idea of the supra-rational knowledge of the Divine and subscribing to Schuon's concept of *Religio Perennis* as an underlying Truth to all religions, Coomaraswamy defined "tradition" as the only source of the spiritual health of humanity.

161

"Metaphysics is not a system," declared Coomaraswamy in his essay on *Vedanta and Western Tradition*, "but a consistent doctrine; it is not merely concerned with conditioned and quantitative experience, but with universal possibility." To Coomaraswamy, metaphysics did not mean a rationalist system or a theological dogma but a mode of knowing where the "knower" and the "known" became one and the same – the same metaphysical process in the empathetic interconnectedness between the Self and the Otherness of the Other. If we take into consideration the "*dogness*" of the dog or the "*treeness*" of the tree when we approach each of these living beings, dualism of the living and the instrumental does not exist anymore. We can think of the tree as a tree and not a resource for making paper. This metaphysical view of the world, as a true form of aesthetic experience of life, has been destroyed, because it is considered as an impediment to the modern development of science and technology.

162

In his essay on *Domestic Handicraft and Culture*, Coomaraswamy tried to articulate the development of techno-science through the example of the gramophone. "No individual ever made a gramophone because he loved music"; he writes, "but the gramophones made in factories are daily destroying the capacity of appreciating real music in the villages." In other words, the mechanical production of the gramophone, where each part is made by a different man and fitted together by another man, destroys the craft tradition of individualized works of art. As a result, Coomaraswamy considers the death of tradition craft and the replacement of small workshop conditions by mechanical production under factory conditions as a sign of the death of culture. As a result, he suggests that "everywhere and always the competition between a man and a machine is destructive of culture" and he adds, "A civilization which cannot effect between them a reasonable division of labor, does not deserve the name."

163

Coomaraswamy does not evaluate civilization in terms of human wants or comfort and safety but as a vocation. In an undated letter written to an anonymous receiver, he explains his concept of civilization and elaborates his critique of modern civilization.

> The effect of our civilization and of industrialism upon any traditional society is to destroy the basis of hereditary vocation on which such societies are based: and we may say that thus to rob the man of his vocation, even though it be done in the name of "liberty," is to rob the man of his "living," not only in an economic sense but in the sense that "man does not live by bread alone"; since it is precisely in such societies that

the professions themselves and for the very reason that the vocation is in every sense of the word natural, provide the solid basis of initiatory teaching.

In other words, for Coomaraswamy, the way of life and the way of work are one and the same, and this is what the traditional societies understood well by including the physical in the spiritual. Thus, Coomaraswamy defines the true artist as a metaphysician who strives to know and to live in the spirit.

164

There is no remedy for our world as long as the nobility of spirit is ignored by masses. Also, no consciousness about the stature of spirit can exist, as long as the Self is cut off from the Otherness of the Other. It was Descartes who exemplified this rupture in his *cogito ergo sum*. The individual consciousness of the thinking subject was proclaimed to be the source of all reality and truth. As a result, Descartes' "*ergo*" does not permit the Otherness of the Other to live in the open. One problem with Descartes' *cogito ergo sum* is that all existence is summed up in "*ergo est.*" That is to say, in modern subject, the communion between the Self and the Otherness of the Other is replaced by the personal idiosyncrasy of the individualistic ego. Maybe that is why we have lost the track of our journey of life.

165

Once the Otherness of the Other becomes our journey, we can better understand the essence of life. But this journey will be costly, if we know *why* and *where* we are going. The Agapeic moment is a moment of suffering, because we are no more an ivory tower witness but a participant in the suffering of the Otherness of the Other. Human beings suffer because they are fragile and mortal and they know that they are fragile and mortal. A dog or a cat suffers biologically and eventually dies, but they don't know why they suffer and die. Which life is better? Living without knowing that one day you shall die or taking one's suffering to the world and announcing it as a leap of faith? One way or another salvation is not guaranteed. Religions are not insurance companies, though the 21st century has turned them into guarantors of redemption.

10   An Ontology of Fragility

166

We, humans, know that we are fragile. Fragility is an essential part of our human condition. There is a common experience of suffering. History is full of sufferings which have been communal. Closer to us are sufferings such as the Holocaust, the Armenian genocide, the Partition of India, the Killing Fields of Cambodia, and the Rwandan ethnic cleansing. Suffering is not beautiful, but it is not repulsive, because it asks for our attention and responsibility. Those who turn their back to the suffering of the Other (be it a cat, a mouse, or a human being) have no capacity to understand it and to fight against it. For we do not seek to understand the Otherness of the Other in order that we may suffer like him or her, but we suffer like him or her in order to understand the Otherness of the Other.

167

Philosophy is a journey of wisdom to change the world. It is a praxis of spiritual emancipation and political education. The greatest philosophy is a philosophy which emphasizes on thinking as a creative mode of being. It is because philosophy is creative thinking that it is interested in something greater than itself, that is the meaning of life. As José Ortega y Gasset points out: "We do not live to think, but, on the contrary, we think in order that we may succeed in surviving." In contrast to the original task of philosophy, today's global world has turned into a meaningless universe of non-thinking and non-acting. As if after 50 centuries of culture, politics, art, and religion, humanity has decided to spend its time in bed watching soap operas and being indifferent to the ecological destruction of the Earth and its own process of idiotization.

DOI: 10.4324/9781003292777-11

168

The real reason behind the twilight of philosophy is its vulgarization and degradation by all those pseudo-philosophers who tried to popularize thinking. According to George Santayana,

> The true philosopher, who is not one chiefly by profession, must be prepared to tread the wine-press alone. He may indeed flourish like the bay-tree in a grateful environment, but more often he will rather resemble a reed shaken by the wind. Whether starved or fed by the accidents of fortune he must find his essential life in his own ideal.

It takes patience to be a philosopher, as it takes faith to be a theologian. Volatile spirits who are looking for celebrity can be neither philosophers nor theologians.

169

The principle of "the greatest happiness of the greatest number" which was made a goal by modern industrial societies exemplifies the rejection of philosophy and philosophers by contemporary societies. True philosophy cannot surrender to conformism and passivity. The function is to criticize reality, not to serve it. Accordingly, the life of philosophy is not a mere accident in the progress of human civilization; it is the very essence of that progress itself. But the creative and critical breath which had stirred the philosophers of ancient Greece no longer inspires the academic philosophers. Those who comprehend the rise of meaninglessness and mediocrity in our global world would recognize in philosophy as critical thinking the reawakening of the conscience of humanity.

170

Philosophical life consists in those moments in which critical reflection not only springs up but also thinks against the tide. Any reflection on the current status of philosophy in today's world cannot avoid an analysis of the relationship between philosophy and life. A critical account of life, as it is lived today, must begin with the unprecedented rise of meaninglessness and mediocrity. The most important triumphs of human mind and action since the Sumerian civilization have entered a profound crisis: societies of the West and the East, which believed they had strong philosophies (either secular or religious) to guide humanity to its salvation suffer from a loss of meaning in their deep convictions. With the post-Cold War changes in the global economic and political spectrums, social media affiliations have been seen as the main elements of cultural and political identification. To seriously address this issue, it is perhaps not enough to acknowledge the crisis of critical rationality, which, in the modern era, served as the guarantor of freedom of expression and civil liberties in the West and the East. Rather, to understand the origin of today's crisis of values, it will be useful to recognize the concurrent phenomenon of the universal domination by the instrumental rationality of capitalism hand in hand with recent technologies.

171

During the past thirty years, instrumental rationality has defined itself as the only truth with a universal and planetary value. This process of valuation only exists because masses around the world believe in a certain regime of truth represented by techno-science. As a result, we are facing a radical mutation that does not happen once and for all in every generation. This mutation is the clear expression of an all-encompassing anti-philosophical movement of corporate mindset that has characterized the Western world and that today has come entirely to the fore. The corporate mindset that dominates the world has shown a tendency to separate knowing from thinking. As such, all that is known is not necessarily thought. Therefore, the question that arises is what is the sense of philosophically oriented thinking in a world where billions are informed by everyday information, but they have lost their capacity to think about their lives? Techno-science is flourishing today and its moralizing attitude is written all over its face.

172

What is philosophy in an age in which people attribute no value to thinking and questioning? How can philosophy understand and confront these difficult times during which mass communication technologies and corporate mindset are not always consistent with democratic norms and the basic moral values which glorify the Otherness of the Other? Perhaps, the time is ripe for philosophy to finally recognize that technological rationality, far from being the opposite of mediocrity or from having definitely left infantilism behind, has instead supported and even presupposed its own relation to the banalization of life. The ability to make promises is what constitutes the nature of technological rationality in its planetary presence in a world without promises. It is through this ability to promise a "better future" that technological rationality controls the fragile existence of human affairs. This creates the possibility for an imperial and arrogant certainty in a world of uncertainties, which exercises its sovereign rule over our daily practices. Progress promised us that our dreams will come true, but it forgot to mention that nightmares are also dreams.

173

Perhaps the task of philosophy today is to make no promises. It would also be its task to nurture the two dimensions of criticality and empathy together to be able to honour and respect the nobility of spirit and the Otherness of the Other. This is perhaps the task of philosophy if it wishes to still have a role in the future of human civilization and the history of the planet Earth. Philosophy is simply a struggle for asking questions that the contemporary world does not want to ask anymore. In this context, the praxis of dissent is not a distant act of refusal which has lost all its subversive and anti-conformist nature. Let us be clear, there is no such thing as a conformist or complacent philosophy. If we talk about philosophy as an art of questioning, we are talking with the same breath about a mode of thinking that can initiate a critical space for negation and for preparing real potentials for balancing and bettering human life. The role of philosophy, therefore, becomes central in opening our eyes to a compelling vision of life and in guiding us to a way that points to a radical transformation of the world.

174

How can we enhance nonviolence through philosophy? This question is very relevant to our contemporary situation, given the violent situation of the world. As it was mentioned previously, nonviolence is the *maxima moralia* of humanity in present times, because it opens the door to the logic of the Otherness of the Other. As an enterprise which begins at the level of thinking, philosophy is not a product of violence. Moreover, even if philosophy thinks about violence and elaborates it conceptually, it cannot practise it as long it remains philosophical. John Dewey defined philosophy as a mode of being whose function is "to free man's mind from bias, and prejudices and to enlarge his perception of the world about him." In other words, philosophy teaches us that thinking is better than fighting, because wisdom is better than ignorance. With this background in mind, we can say that nonviolence makes possible the development of philosophy in all ages and civilizations. As such, both philosophy and nonviolence are essential to the civilizational existence of human beings. Essentially, nonviolence is a worthwhile phenomenon that enables cultures and nations to engage in a dialogue and learn from each other. Nonviolence is an essential mode of being and thinking which opens the door to the Otherness of the Other.

175

Man, since its existence, has always been animated by a mode of thinking which has been either religious, artistic, or philosophical. Philosophy, unlike many other modes of thinking, is a critical thinking which has enforced non-violence. Saying that philosophers were at the origin of systems of thought that have incited violence does not mean that the practice of philosophical reflection is itself violent. This is the main difference between party politics and philosophical teaching. Party politics is about power and sovereignty, whereas philosophy is about reasoning and critical thinking. There is no way we can honour and respect the Otherness of the Other through party politics. Truly speaking, the creation of democracy in ancient Athens and its rebirth in the 18th-century American and French Revolutions is certainly not only the sole work of Athenian, American, and French politicians but also that of Greek philosophers and American and French men of ideas. Since modern representative democracy is the child of the critical awareness of the European mind, the same level of philosophical consciousness is needed in order to rethink contemporary democracy in the mirror of nonviolence.

11 The Meaning of Life

176

As we understand, both philosophy and nonviolence are important for the critical development of contemporary societies and their exit from the age of mediocrity and infantilism. However, this suggestion is not necessarily in tandem with the recommendation of a Plato that, the sovereigns should become philosophers or philosophers become sovereigns. We do not learn and teach philosophy to become sovereigns but to learn how to look at our world, comprehend it, and organize it nonviolently. Fifty centuries of war and peace, civilization and barbarism, art and religion, critical reflection and prejudice have not modified the Aristotelian truth that human beings are *zoon politikon*. Human beings cannot survive outside human societies and communities are always prior to individuals. However, the change is always the fruit of an individual mind. Every individual creates its own meaning of life. But this meaning of life is the sum of every individual's relations with others who came before or who will come after.

177

As Viktor Frankl argues:

> The meaning of life differs from man to man, from day to day, from hour to hour. What matters, therefore, is not the meaning of life in general but rather the specific meaning of a person's life at a given moment. . . . Therein he cannot be replaced, nor can his life be repeated.

As such, each individual is a special being and every living creature is important moment of the stream of life in general. That is why we should be careful not to kill the cockroach or the ant that we encounter by accident. They also might crawl on the same bridge that we are walking upon to cross

DOI: 10.4324/9781003292777-12

the stream of life. There is certainly a lot to learn from the *cockroachness* of a cockroach.

178

Human beings in general have trouble learning from life. Maybe because they live no more in proximity of the Earth and close to the essence of life. This is what Nietzsche claims in his *Also Sprach Zarathustra*: "I beseech you, my brothers, remain faithful to the earth and do not believe those who speak to you of extraterrestrial hopes! They are mixers of poisons whether they know it or not." Today's "mixers of poisons" spend their lives in creating waves in the social media and mass communication. These factories of idiot maker praise individuals who flatter themselves of not knowing about philosophy, culture, and art. No wonder why greatness is no more measured by wisdom, excellence, and moral courage but by the measurement of the house in which we live and our bank account. Consequently, having a permanent income is not a sign of being meaningful.

179

Crowds are blank pages of history. What they leave behind is not engraved in the lives of those who come after. For those who prefer excellence and exemplarity to flattery and bootlicking, the whole history stands as their memorial. Our love of ideas should not lead us to extravagance and wastefulness but to boldness and measuredness. That is why the hero is the person who puts down a line of truth in a republic of lies. A person who knows how to strike a match over the dark reefs of life can also find its balance in the heights of existence. Only this person knows how to be a friend of the Otherness of the Other.

180

There is no way that we could approach the borders of the Otherness of the Other without practising the art of friendship. There is a huge difference between hypocrisy and friendship. A hypocrite is someone who flatters you while believing in its own interest. A friend is someone who criticizes you because every effort towards a new understanding is an asset for the relationship. That is why Nietzsche says that "we should also respect the enemy in our friend." Last but not least, friendship is the common ground of understanding among the Self and the Other beyond the meaningless life of the unprincipled common man. This is where traditions of the East and those of the West come together. Through friendship with other cultures and traditions of thought, we can learn to find ourselves "at home" everywhere. This is when and where we can hear Shiva dancing in heart of the world.

181

The empathetic relation to the Otherness of the Other is not a common form of friendship. We cannot compare with friendship the attraction of the same or different sexes for each other. According to Montaigne:

> Sexual love is but a mad craving for something which escapes us . . . The love of friends is a general universal warmth, temperate moreover and smooth, a warmth which is constant and at rest, all gentleness and evenness, having nothing sharp nor keen.

As soon as we enter the territory of friendship, we can feel what misses in sexual love: moderation and proportion. Aristotle was well aware of this when he talked about friendship as a meaningful moment of life. What interested Aristotle in friendship was the act of togetherness and interconnectedness. In his words:

> In poverty as well as in other misfortunes, people suppose that friends are their only refuge. And friendship is a help to the young, in saving them from error, just as it is also to the old, with a view to the care they require and their diminished capacity for action stemming from their weakness; it is a help also to those in their prime in performing noble actions, for "two going together" are better able to think and to act.

But Aristotle knew well that friendship requires commitment of time and it is based on a trusting relationship. Thus, friendship would have been a much easier relationship in ancient Greece as it is in today's world.

182

The readers of Aristotle know well that for him friendship is a reciprocal relation of goodwill that exists among two individuals who share an interest in each other. Aristotle talks about three forms of shared interest: virtue, pleasure, and utility. None of these shared interests can be a foundation for a relation based on the Otherness of the Other. Also, the friendship in question here is not that of "guest-friendship" (*Xenia*) that we see in Homer's *Iliad*. Hospitality is an ethical attitude which takes into consideration the Other but not necessarily its "Otherness." The friendship we are referring to herewith is *trans-ontological*. It is the dynamic of mixing modes of being. The word *trans-ontological* better expresses the process of empathetic transition from one living creature to another. In addition, it carries with it the idea of the consequent creation of a new understanding of the biological, cultural, and political differences of the Other. The best example of a *trans-ontological* dynamic is expressed in the following poem of Ibn Arabi, the Arab Andalusian Muslim scholar, mystic, poet, and philosopher. Ibn Arabi writes:

> *My heart is open to all winds*
> *It is a pasture for gazelles*
> *And a home for Christian Monks*
> *A temple for idols*
> *The Black Stone of the Mecca Pilgrim*
> *The table of the Torah*
> *And the book of the Koran*
> *Wherever God's caravans turn*
> *The religion of love shall be my religion*
> *And my faith*

183

Truly, it is not really important if Ibn Arabi is a Muslim, a Jew, or a Christian. Even the fact that he is a man of faith is not important. Love and empathy are feelings which transcend faith. Perhaps this is the real test of dialogue and encounter with the Otherness of the Other, where nonviolence as a philosophy of compassion and empathy is also put to the test of reality. The *trans-ontological* friendship provides a strong model of empathetic experience where the Otherness of the Other is perceived and comprehended from its own perspective. A man looking at a cat from the point of view of the "*catness*" of the cat does not consider the cat in the scale of Darwinian evolution but simply as a living being. In such a case, the human spirit of domination and conquest will be replaced by that of empathy, patience, and service.

184

Nature should be no more at the service of Man. It is now Man who needs to be at the service of Nature. Without the presence of Nature, Man's life will be meaningless and chaotic. As Emerson points out, "Nature's darlings, the great, the strong the beautiful, are not children of our law, do not come out of the Sunday School, nor weigh their food, nor punctually keep their commandments." According to Emerson, Nature's strength can make Man strong. As such, Nature and the nobility of Man's spirit are inseparable. For Emerson, "Nature is the symbol of spirit. The whole of Nature is the metaphor of the human mind." One could see Emerson's empathetic vision of Nature as an alternative to a Cartesian view of Nature as a slave of modern Man. Undoubtedly, the view of Man as the absolute master of the planet Earth was amplified in the modern times with the rise of industrial capitalism and technological domination of the environment. As a result, as Nature lost its meaning for Man, life itself became meaningless.

185

Man cannot attain the meaning of life without entering a process of self-realization and spiritual fulfilment. This self-realization is possible only via an empathetic awareness of the Otherness of the Other. As such, the only way to understand and have friendship for another living being is through a process of self-examination and self-exploration which provides life with its deep philosophical meaning. In this process of surrendering its personal ego to the Otherness of the Other, Man is supposed to dedicate life to the principle of harmony of all things. In other words, both life and the world complete each other. With an art of living harmoniously in the world, life itself becomes the soul's permanent abode.

186

If happiness has a meaning, it should be related to the meaning of life itself and not necessarily to the luxuries that we accumulate in everydayness of our life. Once again, life in its substantial meaning is more than living and dying idiotically. There is no question here of salvation or life after death, but the main question is "how" should Man proceed in life in order to be accompanied by the "why" of life? The famous quote of Nietzsche that "He who has a why to live for can bear almost any how" applies here. Accordingly, the aim of life is not to seek the truth but rather to show us the way to stand out of the box of mediocrity. Unfortunately, in the contemporary world, mediocrity and happiness have become equivalent modes of being. All that the society offers to us to create our happiness suffer from a degree of shallowness and mediocrity. As a result, we have abandoned the perspective of having a daunting life in order to live with the laziness and brainlessness of a comfortable life of a follower.

187

Whoever is a follower through and through takes all things superficially even itself. As a result, in order to be happy, one has to become most dishonest to oneself. Happiness, therefore, turns into a form of hypocrisy that does not pronounce its name. Whoever reaches this ideal is remained with no ideal. The irony of our contemporary situation is that we feel like gods without necessarily having a godly ideal. The more meaningless the life we live, the more we have to lower our spirit to be equivalent to it. Perhaps nobody among us can live a heroic moment which can offend our vanity. A man who says: "I like this vanity!" has no reverence for the spirit.

188

A follower, a conformist, a mediocre, a Man of many names, alas, is a being that often runs away from the essence of life. The truth is that anything beyond its shallowness may hurt its vanity. But a heroic soul lives always beyond. What does the word "heroic" mean to us today? Heroes are imagined and shaped by the needs of their socio-cultural contexts. Therefore, a hero can be seen in a variety of ways: as a warrior, a king, a divinity, a lover, or a spiritual character. As the Roman philosopher, Seneca underlines: "We all need someone whose example can regulate our character." In his seminal work *The Hero with a Thousand Faces* published in 1949, Campbell defines a hero as one who battles either personal or historical limitations and who becomes a source through which his society is reborn. Essential to the idea of the mythic hero is that either he or the society in which he lives suffers from some shortcoming. Joseph Campbell describes a hero as a powerful human being who embarks on a quest to win a war, to gain a mystical object, or to gain an understanding, and then returns home with some type of wisdom and self-knowledge. The hero will undergo a series of initiations, tests, or trials. Sometimes this comes with great learning, sometimes with the development of skills. Campbell describes a number of stages or steps along this journey. The first is the Separation/Departure. Destiny calls the hero to his quest. The second stage is the Trials and Victories of Initiation. The final stage of Campbell's hero circle is The Return and Reuniting with society. For Campbell, all great heroic actions, regardless of the culture, can be described in terms of this cycle.

189

In which way could we apply Campbell's model of the hero to our contemporary world? Who are our heroes in today's society? We live in a world of celebrities, not heroes. Achilles, Rama, or Miyamoto Musashi would not have survived in our world. They would have died of shame and humiliation, rather than by violence of a sword. How could a heroic soul celebrate life in a world of meaninglessness where conformism and complacency looms every day? Every real hero is more afraid of being adulated by the ignorant masses than of being ignored by them. For heroism remains a virtue, because as Campbell says, the hero has the "power to bestow boons on his fellow man." The "boon" is spiritual: the hero, once enlightened, promotes enlightenment. The pattern here is that of a universal human mission, an enlightenment, which needs to be accomplished. The hero is the person who knows the way to the Otherness of the Other. This is not only the way of empathy but also the way of a new enlightenment. The noble hero of today is a hero of spirit, not a hero of sword.

190

There are human beings who have not only a nobility of spirit but also a grandeur of heart. They are philosophers of life and death, because they possess the art of living and dying. Life, for them, is a process of Becoming. It's a rare solitude in the heights. It's a noiseless mode of Being and a celebration of life which does not entail violence. In a speech on 20 December 1926, Gandhi affirmed:

> There is nothing on earth that I would not give up for the sake of the country excepting of course two things and two only, namely, truth and nonviolence. I would not sacrifice these two for all the world. For to me Truth is God and there is no way to find Truth except the way of nonviolence. I do not seek to serve India at the sacrifice of Truth or God.

Gandhi strived for something great, too great to be understood by Indian masses or any other populations around the world. That is why a hero like Gandhi knows solitude. He lives and dies with his noble spirit. After all, heroes are men of profound sadness.

12 The Solitude of Nonviolence

191

Almost everything we call "nonviolence" is based on the solitude of one's conscience and its journey of becoming more noble. Cruelty is a tendency which has remained with human beings after five thousand years of civilization. The "monstrous" has not really been tamed, because each time humanity has tried to fight its inner monsters, it has turned to new monstrous postures. Nietzsche had already warned us of the dangers of such a process. Humanity has not been able to get rid of its evils. Prophets, saints, philosophers, and poets have taken much trouble throughout history to remind us of the threatening ills and evils of humankind, but they have always been slandered, extradited, sent into exile, or crucified. It has always been hard to preach for men of mediocrity.

192

Nonviolence has always been a displeasing idea for mediocre masses, who would rather watch a scene of hanging rather than reading a page of Homer. The killing instincts of individuals who have never suffered profoundly determines their rank in the moral order of the universe. Even a squirrel never wishes the death of another squirrel in order to gather all the nuts for its own good. But mass men cannot stand each other's smell. Could it be that nobility of spirit is the exception and not the rule? This is not what the philosophy of nonviolence teaches us. Undoubtedly, individuals such as Zoroaster, the Buddha, Jesus Christ, Saint Francis, Gandhi, and Martin Luther King, Jr. believed that there is a cure for every poison, as long as human beings realize that they have created it.

DOI: 10.4324/9781003292777-13

193

The pursuit of an ideal is central to the make-up of the modern hero and like the Homeric hero, there are no limits to achieving the goals the hero must accomplish. In striving to achieve his objectives, the hero will have to make personal sacrifices and even offer its life to the cause it believes in. Such a choice is in the heroic manner; one might even say, more pertinently, in the manner of a Homeric hero like Odysseus or Achilles. While on the one hand this may be true of Gandhi and King as modern heroes, the complexity of deconstructing them as heroes is the fact that they do not in many respects embody the characteristics associated with the Homeric hero. They were not physically strong, did not have slightly overblown egos, and were not vengeful, but like Odysseus, they were heroes of persuasion and stratagem.

194

Thomas Carlyle's *On Heroes, Hero-Worship, and The Heroic in History* taught Gandhi of the greatness, bravery, and humility of prophets. We can find examples of Gandhi and King's humility in their selfless sacrifice for the cause of nonviolence. Gandhi and King put themselves at risk in particular situations for the benefit of specific opponents, but they were aware that their self-sacrifice was also reaching beyond the particular places where they stood. In the case of Gandhi and King, nonviolent self-sacrifice goes hand in hand with self-transformation. Both Gandhi and King struggled with their own transformation as nonviolent heroes. According to Gandhi, a *Satyagrahi* had to participate in Truth and Truth "could not depend on individual impressions and decisions alone." It had to be extraordinarily disciplined, with a "commitment to suffer the opponent's anger without getting angry and yet also without ever submitting to any violent coercion."

195

Satyagraha is defined by Gandhi as redemptive and transformative. King also recognized the need for spiritual transformation. King's mythical journey portrays a hero who has made sacrifices. King's most famous oration, *"I Have a Dream,"* also refers to the suffering encountered by him. King uses his periodic jailing as a metaphor for the isolation of segregation. King's rhetoric works to produce an image of sacrifice and suffering when he says:

> I am not unmindful that some of you have come fresh from narrow jail cells. Some of you have come from areas where your quest for freedom

left you battered by the storms of persecution and staggered by the winds of police brutality.

Gandhi and King's heroic nonviolence is, therefore, a strategy for action and an active commitment to caring for the Otherness of the Other. In other words, in Gandhian nonviolence, the idea of heroic entails participation among the non-heroic. It is willingness to go to any length to restore a compassionate and empathetic community.

196

Undoubtedly, a nonviolent hero is always lonely, but its loneliness is a necessary mode of being. Maybe because the life of a nonviolent hero can only be lived in loneliness, but it must be achieved with and for others. The nonviolent hero acts on the behalf of the Otherness of the Other. Deep within the lonely soul of the nonviolent hero lies the concept of empathy, which evokes an epic sense of the moral heroism of nonviolent struggle. As a result, a lonely life in nonviolence turns into a sweet drink, and yet it must be taken in drops. These are drops of excellence and exemplarity. The nonviolent hero chooses one thing: always to have exemplarity on its side. It believes in a life of autonomous thinking but nonetheless a life with role models. It can never be said enough that today's world is full of celebrities and void of role models.

197

Seneca advised Romans to "turn to better men: live with the Catos, with Laelius, with Tubero. But if it pleases you to live with the Greeks also, associate with Socrates, with Zeno." *Exempla* are no more present in our everyday life. Who are the *exempla* that could cast a long shadow over our meaningless lives today? Actually, the *exemplum* is nonviolence itself, as a promise of empathy that makes a certain future possible. This is a future that listens to the past and learns from it, but it is the possibility of a meaningful life and a history experienced from the perspective of the Otherness of the Other. By self-consciously cultivating an ethical exemplarity, Gandhian nonviolence testifies to the dialogical fellowship of the Self with the Otherness of the Other. Here the relation with the Otherness of the Other is inseparable from the transformative Becoming of the Self in the process of nonviolent action. The Other can be anything whatsoever or anyone whosoever, but the nonviolent strategy of the Self remains in all situations empathetic and self-transformative.

198

It is from this self-transformative possibility that the Gandhian nonviolence has the capacity to think differently about the act of thinking and the art of acting. Moreover, as an ethical imperative, the Otherness of the Other is unconditional, not because it is an ideal but because it is a principle of cosmic fellowship. As such, empathy is nothing but the affirmative experience of the Otherness of the Other. It is also nonviolence as the nonviolence-to-come. The future remains an open possibility because of the dignity of the Otherness of the Other. It is here that the ethical and the political come together in the Gandhian logic of nonviolent thinking. To be sure, what the Gandhian nonviolence acknowledges is the ethical content of civilization but also indicates the historical barriers to this. After all, how can a people pretend to be civilized and dismiss the question of the Otherness of the Other?

199

What does it mean to be civilized? Who is civilized and how do we distinguish a civilized person from what is considered as "uncivilized"? As history shows us, the sacralization of the idea of civilization and its enforcement beyond the borders of a nation or a culture have always been accompanied by an exclusivist temperance which has dismissed and discarded the Otherness of the Other. As a result, modernity and its project of a unique civilization were achieved through a logic of bellicose truth, which saw the emergence of a new historical process of domination of the Otherness of the Other. As a result, the modern crusade for civility generated a range of mechanisms that shaped the subjectivity of the Western Man but annihilated that of the Others. The process of ordering the Otherness of the Other implied a dynamic of taming and disciplining rather than communicating and interconnecting. Thus, central to the process of "civilizing" at home and abroad was the destruction of the Otherness of the Other.

200

An individual or a nation which always takes pride in being "civilized" will always try to be "uncivilized." For civilizations are sometimes judged wrongly by those who consider them too civilized. A civilization that does not know how to ask for forgiveness takes a pleasure in humiliation the Otherness of the Other. Sadeq Khalkhali, the hanging judge of the Iranian Revolution, was also a cat killer, but he never asked forgiveness for killing cats. Civilizations are full of uncivilized characters.

201

Today's global society shines bright only when the ray of the "civilizing process" falls on it; otherwise, it is overflowing with dark clouds. Plants need light, not lies. Humans can accommodate themselves with lies and continue living with the myth of *glamour* and *brightness*. They submit from habit to anything that gives them the illusion of being powerful and important. But to be "civilized" one needs to be spirited and empathetic. As such, civilization is neither the expression of humankind's power nor that of its madness, but an exemplification of Man's own battle with rapacity and avidity. These days, of course, we admire the gospel of selfishness and meanness. Never has life been so meaningless in the social realm and lived so inhumanely in present history. The distance that separates us from the *Funeral Oration* of Pericles is not only historical but also ontological.

202

In his speech, taken up by Thucydides, Pericles pays homage to the Athenian soldiers who died in the Peloponnesian War and praises the merits of the Athenian model of governing for other Greek cities. In his *Funeral Oration*, Pericles talks not only about democracy and war but also of the love of beauty among Athenian citizens. Pericles declares: *"Philokaloumen gar met'euteleias kai philsophoumen aneu malakias* – we love beauty without ostentation and we love wisdom without being soft." We can add here the commentary of Cornelius Castoriadis:

> Pericles does not say we love beautiful things (and put them in museums), we love wisdom (and pay professors or buy books). He says we *are* in and by the love of beauty and wisdom and the activity this love brings forth, we live by and with and through them – but far from extravagance, and far from flabbiness . . . The object of the institution of the *polis* is for [Pericles] the creation of a human being, the Athenian citizen, who exists and lives in and through the unity of these three: the love and "practice" of beauty, the love and "practice" of wisdom, the care and responsibility for the common good, the collectivity, the *polis.* . . . Among the three there can be no separation; beauty and wisdom such as the Athenians loved them and lived them could only exist in Athens. The Athenian citizen is not a "private philosopher," or a "private artist," he is a citizen for whom philosophy and art have become ways of life.

203

The value of a civilization is in the mode of thinking and the way of life of its citizens. Today's civilization does not educate its children with beauty and wisdom. It provides them shallowness, banality, and mediocrity. In such a highly technologically developed civilization, human beings cannot think. They only express opinions about everything by imitating great thinkers of the past with a perfect art of deception. Complete deceitfulness in thought and inquiry, that is mediocracy, has become a quality of character in our societies. One can promise here greed for money, lust for power, and thirst for fame but assuredly no passion for beauty and no love for wisdom.

204

Thinking of the Otherness of the Other is the coming of age of human civilization. Irrespective of its historical connotations, civilization has been an idea that constitutes a relationship in which human beings relate to each other, and this relationship is best represented by the idea of living together. Living together is essentially a civilizational dynamic that allows human subjects to know themselves and others, thereby helping in their self-realization. Compassion and empathy have been the defining principles of civilization re-enforced by a common humanity. Unlike what the common people think in some countries, no civilization can advance at the expense of the Otherness of the Other. In other words, every civilization must have an ethical goal, a kernel of what our future ought to be. Without this ethical goal, civilization is meaningless and directionless and therefore de-civilizing. As a matter of fact, the real battle of civilization is not among civilizations but for the survival of civilization as the time and space of the Otherness of the Other.

205

The fear of the Other and its Otherness remains a civilizational truth. However, ethics of empathy continues to serve as a key to the embracement, inclusion, and recognition of the Otherness of the Other. It is because of this ethics of empathy toward the Other and the act of recognition of its Otherness that human beings can transcend the violence contained in the pages of history. Unfortunately, modern civilization has disturbed this equation by making human beings dependent on material progress and technologies, and political institutions at the cost of moral progress and interconnectedness of human beings with the essence of life itself. It is, therefore, time for us to differentiate moral progress from material progress and to argue for the permanence and persistence of the former. Thus, in today's de-civilized world, taking into account the Otherness of the Other brings a fresh life to the idea of cosmic fellowship, by subjecting our thoughtless civilization to ethical test.

206

It's time for us to put greater emphasis on the ethical character of our human civilization, a criterion for apprehending the Otherness of the Other. This helps us to recognize that ontological differences and diversities can never be done away with. As Charlie Chaplin used to say: "Life is a beautiful magnificent thing, even to a jellyfish." The whole point for us, human beings, is to be able to have *a jellyfish moment*, while remaining human. If this would have been possible, we would not have been conquerors and destroyers of the universe but listeners and learners of the world. For such a transformation we need to look within ourselves for the little bit of jellyfish that we all have, the capacity to have life and to turn our back to the three "Ps": pretension, pride, and prejudice. We can only hope that the nobility of human spirit would never decline at a point that it would cherish no more love, compassion, and empathy, the three essential paths to the Otherness of the Other and exit from the age of mediocrity.

Index

For Product Safety Concerns and Information please contact our EU
representative GPSR@taylorandfrancis.com Taylor & Francis Verlag GmbH,
Kaufingerstraße 24, 80331 München, Germany

Batch number: 08153772

Printed by Printforce, the Netherlands